Foreword

Coaches, gurus, bloggers and vloggers are a dime a dozen. These days, everyone's got something to say. <u>Most are not worth hearing</u>.

Mike Marchev is worth listening to. Listen to Mike.

When he talks about growing and managing a vibrant business, his messages are clear, concise, practical and achievable.

Have you ever spent time with Mike? I have. His presence changes me, each and every time. It happens when I am standing back-of-house watching him deliver a powerfully compelling keynote. It happens when we spend time together on the phone - sharing and laughing about business and life. It happened when we once spent ten days together on a 55-foot catamaran that he personally captained through the British Virgin Islands. I was lucky enough to be one of his crew.

I listen to Mike because he is a man of profound wit and wisdom. A competitor. And, a dear friend. Among my closest.

How happy am I that he composed this bedtime story book filled with some of his best stories and messages? Exceedingly excited.

It is an essential read for me, and I trust it will be for you also. It'll give you an opportunity to spend time with Mike as he writes exactly like he talks. It will be like you are sitting across from him.

He is a beacon! Come get some light.
I'll close with one small adjustment to one of Mike's classic quotes:

"There are two kinds of people in the world. People who can help you, and people who can't."

Listen to Mike. He is a person who can help you. I know he has helped me.

Stuart Lloyd Cohen

Chief Motivation Officer

A Message From Mike ... *Before Beginning Your Journey*

To avoid any misunderstandings just prior to your turning out the lights I want to make it clear that this book is not about Little Bo Peep, Cinderella or The Three Little Pigs. There will be no reference to The Little Engine That Could, Snow White or Pinocchio.

But now that I think about it, there are quite a few similarities that could dove-tail with a few messages and reminders in each and every one of these night-time "reminders."

The stories you are about to be introduced have **YOU** as the main character. And each and every "story" has been designed to (1) get you thinking, (2) remind you of a long-forgotten business-development lesson, and/or (3) introduce you to a new concept worth considering.

This "anthology" was not intended to be read in a linear fashion. It certainly was not written that way. Those who know me realize I chose to take a more circuitous path through life. Each of these stories can stand on its own. Glance down through the Table of Contents and pick a title that catches your attention. To the best of my knowledge, there is no "fluff" in my stories. They deliver a message you can take to the bank. Interpret them as you wish. Make them your own. Read them more than once.

And one more thing before you turn the page. Your success will not come by accident or without your involvement. Little-by-little, step-by-step, you will be rewarded for your efforts if and when you consistently and persistently pursue your goals.

I want to remind you that one year from today you will be the same person you are at this very moment except for the people you hang out with and the books you read. I can virtually guarantee you that if you read *and internalize* just one story each night for the next 100 nights, you will be miles ahead of your competition in a little more than three months. As for the people you choose to hang out with, I am afraid I have to leave that to your good judgement.

One story each night. Begin tonight. Tomorrow is the day your life begins to change.

Table of Contents

1. Who's Next?...7
2. The Ideal Sales Strategy 9
3. Stuff Happens 10
4. Be Happening! 11
5. Selling Is No Longer A "Numbers Game"..12
6. Who Said You Have to Like "Everybody?"..14
7. Believe It Or Not, Stress Is An Option 16
8. Marketing Works ... But Only If You Do 17
9. Respond To Leads Promptly...18
10. TGIT: Thank Goodness It's Today! 19
11. Sometimes Things Actually Do Work 20
12. Stop. Think. Observe. Act...21
13. It Isn't Over Until It Is Over 22
14. Your Tone Speaks Volumes 23
15. You Market For Tomorrow...25
16. You Didn't Get This Far By Accident!..26
17. The Importance of Leading a Disciplined Life...27
18. Take Responsibility For Your Future...28
19. Multitasking Is a Game For Clowns 29
20. A Gentle "Wake Up Call" Might Be In Order 30
21. Clarity of Intention 31
22. Are You Doing Enough "Laughing & Scratching?" 32
23. Stop Worrying And Hit The Ball...33
24. A Lesson From Your Morning Crossword Puzzle 34
25. Read That Book Again 35
26. Books And Crossword Puzzles: Part 2 36
27. Don't Stop Thinking About Tomorrow..37
28. Elephants Don't Bite..38
29. Failure Is Not Something To Avoid 39
30. I Love It When a Plan Comes Together..40

31. You Can't Tell a Book By Its Cover...42
32. The Next One Could Be The Big One..43
33. Podcasts "R" Us 44
34. Simple Is Better 45
35. Some Ideas Are Worth Repeating 46
36. There's No Such Thing As "Down-Time" 47
37. The Path To Success Is Usually Less Traveled 48
38. Nobody Owes You a Living 50
39. Don't Bite Off More Than You Can Chew 51
40. Choose Your Words Wisely 52
41. Execution 53
42. Marketing Strategy # 7: The Interview 54
43. Lessons From A Fabric Store 56
44. Are You Climbing Up The Wrong Ladder? 57
45. Repetition Is Not a Bad Thing 58
46. Are You Protecting Your Greatest Asset? 59
47. Don't "Throw In The Towel?" Not Yet! 60
48. Three "Brilliant" Reminders 62
49. Some Good Advice For Job Seekers 64
50. Did Somebody Say "Attunement?"..66
51. In Search Of That Elusive "One Thing" 67
52. From Annoying Pest To Welcome Guest 68
53. Follow Up Never Goes Out of Style...69
54. What Does a Clogged Gutter Have To Do With Anything? 71
55. My Thoughts On Integrity Selling..72
56. "Lazy" Is Not a Flattering Characteristic..73
57. Are You Becoming Lazy? Part Two 74
58. The Good Ole Days Are Still Ahead 75
59. "Flying Around The Water Tower" 76
60. Marketing Is Not For The Lazy 77
61. "The Hay Is In The Barn" 78

62. The "Deadliest" Sales Mistake 79
63. Your Real "A" List 81
64. People Are Watching. ("Walk Your Talk") 82
65. Small Wins Lead To Big Results 83
66. It Is Better Together 84
67. Take Time To Count Your Blessings 85
68. You Can Start Tomorrow? 86
69. Is Your Quality Controlled? 87
70. A Lesson Worth Repeating 88
71. Tell Me The Truth! 90
72. We Are Just Human! 91
73. "Fine" Is Never Good Enough 92
74. Lessons From A Former Quarterback 93
75. Your "Tone" Speaks Volumes 94
76. A Note To Myself 96
77. FCS: These Three Letters Will Help Run Your Business 97
78. Pick Up The Phone. Make The Call. 98
79. Pretty Close To a Proven Success Formula 99
80. Five Customer Service Reminders 100
81. Final Day of The Proven Success Formula: Motivation 101
82. What Does Calking a Bathroom Seam Have To Do With You? 102
83. Mediocrity Is Not a Good Thing 103
84. The Power of The Well-Executed "Launch" 104
85. Kaizen Revisited 105
86. Don't Sell "Snail Mail" Short 106
87. It Is Time That You Make Your Move 107
88. "I Know You're Busy So I'll Let You Go!" 108
89. Ready Or Not Here Comes Tomorrow. 109
90. Would've - Could've - Should've 110
91. The Four D's. (Four Words Leading To Your Success) 111
92. Get Yourself In Position To Win 113

93. *You Had Me At "Hello!"* 114
94. *Who Remembers The "E-Ticket?"* 116
95. *What Are You Waiting For?* 118
96. *Playing Tentatively Is For Losers* 120
97. *Nobody Cares About You!* 121
98. *Podcasts Have Become "The Talk Of the Town"* 123
99. *Playing It Safe May Not Be Your Best Move* 124
100. *"You've Got This!"* 125
My Final Words! 127
Mike's Bio 128

1. Who's Next?

There is one thing travel entrepreneurs can never lose sight of. **What is true today may not be true tomorrow.** If this past year has taught us anything, it is this: Change is inevitable. Stuff happens. Yesterday's news is exactly that ... yesterday's news. How you choose to spend your time tomorrow will determine the resultant smile on your face as you move forward.

Here is another fact we can agree with. There is no shortage of *advice* coming from the mouths, offices and websites of self-labeled industry gurus.

But getting back to the title of tonight's story, "Who's next?"

Regardless of your current situation, if I were asked for a one word answer it would sound a lot like "prospecting." **Prospecting** will always be the key to your business success. I suppose another two words that support this task would be **"Lead Generation."**

PRE-REQUISITE: Before spending your time trying to uncover new business opportunities, you would be well-advised to solidify the relationships you already have with your "valued" clients. Remember, your customer is my prospect. Protect your current assets.

FACT: The sooner you internalize the importance of seeking new business opportunities, the sooner you will be sowing the seeds for a profitable future. *(But not before you re-read the pre-requisite paragraph above.)*

Back To Prospecting.

To help you simplify this prospecting thing, you can divide the population of our planet into two categories. Over seven billion people reside on our planet, and you can divide them into two groups.

Group 1: People you can help.   **Group 2: People you can't help.**

Once you begin looking at your personal marketplace through this new lens, your job will immediately make sense to you.

Your job becomes identifying individuals you can help. How you choose to do this is up to you, but I believe the most efficient way is by trying to find out who has a genuine interest in your particular area of expertise. Get "prospects" to raise their hand indicating interest in you and your topic. Then supply them with valuable information designed to satisfy their curiosity "scratch their itch."

You can use your phone, email, snail mail, or meet with groups of people to ask them if they would like to learn more about your specialty. If this sounds too simplistic then you are reading me correctly. It sounds simple because it is simple. It is simple because it is logical.

Personally, I offer a "Special Report" to accomplish this task. It might sound something like this: ***"If you would like to learn how you can double your business in the next twelve months (really) I have a document you might want to read. It is titled My 12-Word Marketing Plan."*** *(That is step #1.)*

Readers who send me an email requesting my report are clearly indicating they are interested in learning how to expand their client base. They are raising their hand and voluntarily positioning themselves as potential prospects.

(Step #2.) I send them the requested information giving them a written document to judge me by. They get a feel for my personality along with my knowledge of the subject matter and my communication style. I follow up giving them time to internalize my information. Eventually something will happen. By "something" I mean either a budding relationship results, or I realize they are not interested in me or the horse I rode in on. I classify them accordingly, and file their contact information.

If there is a secret to this prospecting thing it is to do it daily, regularly... and consistently. Keep your eyes and ears open for opportunities where you can ask ***"Are you interested in learning more about..."***

You will be sabotaging your efforts if you (1) postpone your prospecting campaign, or (2) initiate a hit or miss program with days, weeks, or months between inactivity.

I'm telling you your next "profitable" client is out there. You just have to go find them. You must keep looking. You must not stop looking until you find them. They are out there. Honest!

Now get yourself a good night's sleep. The hard part is over. You have begun reading 100 Bedtime Stories For Travel Professionals. Only 99 to go. Clear your mind of excess clutter and tomorrow you can start your prospecting campaign with a fresh game plan. (But not before you cement your current relationship with your good clients.)

2. The Ideal Sales Strategy

The state was New Mexico. The time was a few years back. The place was an automobile dealership.

I was invited to share a few of my ideas and proven selling tactics to a room full of professional salespeople. Their monthly sales goal was to sell 300 cars every month. (Every month.) It was clear to me that I was not speaking to room full of amateurs.

What caught my curiosity was that every person in the room carried a silver coin in their pocket reminding them that they were the best in the business. The one-word engraved on the coin was **Loyalty**.

This word was driven home in every sales meeting and their single objective was to maintain their current customer list for a long time. Their goal might have been 300 cars, but their results were determined by how well their current clients were treated.

TREAT YOUR CLIENTS AS IF THEY HOLD THE KEYS TO YOUR FUTURE ...
because they do.

We often treat our neighbor's children with more respect than we treat our own children. We are often more polite to strangers than we are to our loved ones. We go out of our way for prospects more readily than we reach out to our valued clients. This is strange behavior no matter how you slice it.

The winners in a winning organization are the customers. They need to be treated as if the company sincerely wants them to return.

Tonight's message:

Focus on the needs of your current client base and make it your business to hold on to every single one. Build your business based on a 100% satisfaction level of those you are currently doing business with.

Customer loyalty is fast becoming a thing of the past. Just like my new friends in New Mexico, do not allow this to happen to you. Hold onto your loyal clients and don't ever let them go.

****You might want to do yourself a favor by selecting a reminder of your own and carry it with you to remind you throughout the day that customers are King.

3. Stuff Happens

Summer thunderstorms have a way of creating havoc. One minute you have electricity and your TV is working as designed. In a blink of an eye and without warning you find yourself powerless. (Without juice.) BAM! Lights out.

This is another example of how quickly things change... and can change ... and do change ... and will change. One minute you are sailing nicely downwind and before you can say "coming about" you are sitting "high and dry" on a sandbar. One minute you have all the business you can handle; the next your pipeline is drier than an Arizona summer's day. One minute life is grand...then your upcoming weekend becomes disrupted with an unexpected phone call from a distant relative. (You get my drift.)

Stuff happens. The lights went out in Georgia... and you could be next. As a matter fact, you should count on it. Someday... one day... your lights will go out. My question to you is will you be prepared to handle it like the professional you claim to be?

Ask yourself "what is the **absolute worst thing** that could happen to me in the next few days, weeks, months?" Then do everything in your power to make certain it doesn't happen.

Here are a few examples to help stimulate your preparation.

Worse Thing?	What you can do now
Pulled back muscle	Stretch more often (daily)
Lost account	Call them now and ask to catch up
Spouse leaves you	Roses, dinner and a few heartfelt romantic words
Kid gets on drugs	Take in a ballgame and show interest in their opinions
Get fired (1)	Get to work earlier. Stop whining
Get fired (2)	Begin networking campaign. Update your resume
Get fired (3)	Celebrate
A blackout	Buy batteries and another flashlight...today.
Roof leaks	Patch and replace ASAP
Pets run away	Fix hole in the fence
You trip in the garage	Clean it up once and for all. Stop procrastinating.
You can't find key papers	Organize and clean your files...pronto.

You don't have to be caught in the dark if you just exercise a little emotional intelligence. Just do everything you can today to make sure bad "stuff" does not happen to you tomorrow. This simple exercise will position you as a truly exceptional person.

PS. To avoid losing your business as result of a computer crash, back up your important files today. ***And store them off property***.

4. Be Happening!

A few years back I visited my high school to spend a day with the senior class. One of my main messages was a recommendation to avoid negative people at all cost. No truer words have ever been spoken. *"Misery loves company."* Do not fall into the web of down-trodden, whining, bummed-out, woe is me, life is unfair individuals. The world has its share of people who prefer to be the victim. Don't just walk away from these people ... ***RUN AWAY.***

The flip side to this advice it is to migrate toward **happening** people. When you come across a person full of ideas who is not frightened to try new things, make an attempt to hitch your wagon to these stabilizing forces and be open to explore the possibilities.

The power of positive people, positive views, and positive comments is an uplifting phenomenon. Talking to a positive person on the phone or enjoying a few minutes of their company has a tendency to lift one's spirits. Just yesterday I spent time with an 85-year-old woman, (high heels and all,) who had the mind and quick wit of today's 20-year-old. Our time together was both refreshing and invigorating. (My wife's aunt.)

I have a number of associates I contact on a regular basis. Before long I find myself laughing, cajoling and brainstorming myself right out of a less-than-positive mood. It works every time.

So, if you find yourself heading for "***Rutsville***" make a call to a member of your "A-Team" and ***snap out of it***. We are all in this thing together, and we will all get out of this thing together. Try something new. Attempt something bold. **BE HAPPENING!**

One more thing before you turn out the lights. When somebody calls you it may be a disguised call for help ... an opportunity to pump some life back into their world. Answer the phone tomorrow like you have it together. There are people out there who need you. They could be counting on you to help lift their spirits. Don't let them down. Nobody is better at this than you.

Starting tomorrow begin showcasing the brand new "*HAPPENING*" you.

5. Selling Is No Longer A "Numbers Game"

Selling was once believed to be a numbers game. You have undoubtedly heard this popular, weather-beaten sales advice before. **Make the calls. Make the presentations. Work your way through enough people, and eventually you will make a sale**. I'm quick to admit this is not totally false. Raw volume, however, does not necessarily produce success. And even if it did, it would do nothing to enhance your professional reputation.

Rather than thinking of sales as a game of numbers, I want you to begin thinking of sales as **"a game of darts."** By aiming your effort (the dart) at a clearly defined target (your pre-qualified prospect dart board) your chances for hitting the mark (a sale) are greatly enhanced. Contrast that mindset with a pure numbers game where you buy a lottery ticket on a "whim and a prayer" or you throw a handful of marbles up in the air hoping one or two land in a paper cup twenty feet away.

If you want to save yourself a lot of time, money and frustration, have an idea of who you would like to do business with. That's right. I want you to identify your target audience. Your chance for success is much higher if you direct your efforts conscientiously toward a list of defined prospects. This concept is known as "Target Marketing."

Example:
Tell me you want to do business with the Pastor of your church, Reverend Genuflect; your local wine merchant Mr. Chardonnay; The couple down the street, Mary and Tyler what's-their-name?

To help explain the concept, I will refer to the process as "bracketing." Bracketing is a systematic approach for zeroing in on a designated target. Let's use a golfing example of bracketing in action.

During a Merrill Lynch corporate golf outing I once monitored in Tucson, Arizona, Al Geiberger was the guest PGA golf professional. He was positioned on a Par 3 hole as each foursome of company representatives played through. Al's job as the guest pro was to hit a fifth ball on behalf of each team to win a "closest-to-the-pin" prize.

Prior to the first group arriving at the designated hole, I saw Al hit a single shot to check the distance, wind and firmness of the green. (He was firing his first shot to get a lay of the land.) His initial attempt fell short and to the left of the flagstick. Mr. Geiberger mentally recorded the results. After making a few mechanical adjustments he hit a second ball and watched its flight. This time the ball landed a little long and to the right of the flagstick. Again, he adjusted his mechanics. His third shot was pin high and left. After making the final adjustment, his fourth shot was right on the money. After mentally recording and locking in the swing mechanics for shot #4, he duplicated the shot all afternoon coming within a few feet of the hole. This impressed the bejabbers out of each passing foursome.

This is how bracketing works — a trial and error, adjustment setting exercise designed to zero in on a given target. Bracketing in sales works the same way. First, you have to lob some effort in the direction of a specific goal (your specified prospect). Then pay attention to what happens. Make a necessary adjustment and try it again. Keep on tweaking your strategy until you identify a method that results in the prospect becoming a client.

While I have your attention, here is a sales exercise you can experiment with:

(1) Make a list of five qualified prospects you would like to do business with.

(2) Write down three ways you can initiate awareness of your products or services among these prospects.

(3) Initiate your awareness program and record your results from the first-round attempt.

(4) Make your necessary adjustments to the program and try again (either on the same five prospects or on a new set of five).

(5) Record and adjust again. Continue until you are, as the pros say, in the zone.

(6) Finally, apply your refined method to a new group of targeted prospects.

Caution: Bracketing will not effectively work with prospects you have not qualified. Shooting from the hip will have you playing the old lottery numbers game. Trying to bracket unqualified prospects is like Al Geiberger trying to drop his shot near the hole when the winds gust to 40 miles per hour coming from a different direction at any given time. Similarly, unqualified prospects are coming from all different directions in terms of what they want and need. You'll miss the _**green**_ and become discouraged in no time.

Starting tomorrow, allow others to waste their time chasing raw numbers. Identify your target and with bracketing as your guiding strategy, become successful by design. There will be very little luck to your new sales campaign. **(Lights out.)**

6. Who Said You Have to Like "Everybody?"

Tonight, I'm going to introduce you to a popular sales myth. Bear with me on this one since it may rub you the wrong way at first. I think you will soon be agreeing with me.

Many people preach that a prerequisite for becoming successful in sales is to "like people." The implication here is you should have the innate capacity and desire to cozy up to just about anybody who can fog a mirror . . . or at least anybody with a fat wallet. I am not a fan of this postulate. Let me explain.

I have traversed the United States many times, worked in nineteen countries on five continents, and observed countless people on airplanes, in post office lines, at restaurants, toll booths, and department store customer service counters. I have watched people drive cars, run races, attend classes, and root for their kids at high school athletic programs. For over seventy years I have watched people do just about everything people can conceivably do on this planet. (Well . . . almost everything.)

Here is what I have concluded: The world has its quota of boring, insincere, self-centered and negative people who I consciously choose to have nothing to do with. More accurately stated, I don't like them or endorse what they stand for. I have no intention or desire of entering their world or trying to change them.

On the other hand, during these same travels, I have met many fine, upstanding, fun and creative human beings trying to creatively figure out how things work while maintaining a refreshing sense of humor and appreciation for life itself. These people are the ones I choose to be around . . . learn from . . . and try to emulate. I like these people. The point I am trying to make is ***I like the people I like***.

Let's give this "you've got to like people" a slightly different twist. If you want to minimize your stress, have more fun and earn more money, begin spending more time looking for, and doing business with, people you have a natural attraction for . . . people who are honest, hardworking, fun, intelligent, enthusiastic and easy to be around.

It does make sense however, to take a little time to understand people better. After all, many nice people just don't know how to make a good first impression. It would be a shame for you to prematurely cross them off your list simply because they are having a bad hair day.

You may feel a little out of joint right now and be saying to yourself, "Is this guy saying that it is okay to be prejudiced?" No! Not at all. Take a deep breath and read the above paragraphs again. I am saying that it is okay if you choose not to do business with rude, unhappy, belly- aching whiners. That is what I am saying, and I will say it in a court of law if you insist on hearing it under oath.

Where does it say you must do business with (or worse, seek business from) everyone who wants your service or product? That's a myth.

If you are going to service people to the full extent of your capabilities, you might as well do it for people who appreciate your contributions and hard work. This alone will result in more energy and a positive attitude. And that my friends translates to a happier you and a more successful business.

Beginning tomorrow, start identifying the people you like to be around. And while you are at it, start focusing on ways you can become more likeable.

7. Believe It Or Not, Stress Is An Option

Another myth often associated with the selling profession is that stress, like rejection, is inevitable. It is true the two often "travel" together weighing down the carrier. The truth also is that stress is not absolutely necessary.

Without exception everyone acknowledges they experience some level of stress in their lives. They seem to accept stress as a common debilitation given at birth, and they often have been heard bragging about it. (Strange behavior.)

It's true that a lot of sales professionals exhibit stress at times. But stress does not have to rule your life. You were not born with stress, like the color of your eyes. It is something that you allow to happen along life's circuitous path. Stress is self-imposed in many if not most cases and is a by-product of pretending that the world operates differently than it actually does.

When our imperfect world, on whose game board we all must function follows its natural course, we object to its imperfections and thereby fuel our personal stress level. In engineering, stress results from the application of a constant force to an immovable object. In life, the force is your **expectations**. The object is **reality**. You pretend . . . you guess wrong . . . you get stressed. Once you learn to go with the natural flow and rhythms of the world (by all means stopping long enough to change what can be changed), you will become more effective, efficient and pleasant to be around.

Starting tomorrow, begin accepting our imperfect world for what it is ... imperfect. Change what you can but stop becoming befuddled with what you have no control over.

8. Marketing Works ... *But Only If You Do*

I don't consider myself an impulse buyer, but I once purchased a vacuum cleaner from a TV infomercial .... *at 3:30 am*.

I am usually asleep at 3:30 am, but on this particular night in a Kansas City hotel I found it difficult to fall asleep. I was wide awake watching television when an infomercial caught my attention. Before I knew it, I was the proud owner of a vacuum cleaner known as ***The Stick Shark***. This thing sucks up screws and bolts like nothing you have ever seen. *How did that happen?*

Later that week...
I read about a new book titled **The Tipping Point** in the New York Times, by Malcolm Gladwell. It looked like something I might be interested in, but I didn't give it another thought ... until I was browsing at Barnes & Noble on Saturday afternoon and I spotted it in the business section. I was soon reading **The Tipping Point**. *How did that happen?*

In both instances, "it" happened because the product was brought to my attention. In both instances, a product was introduced, and I was given a few reasons why I might want to consider buying the product. I was not shopping for a vacuum cleaner nor does my office library need another business book. It wasn't my idea to purchase either of these products ... until the product was brought to my attention.

These are two examples of how marketing works. Granted, it doesn't work all the time on every single prospect, but in the long run, it works. But I can promise you that it won't work unless you do. **And here is what you have to do**.

1. You must introduce yourself and your service to targeted people in your marketplace. In the majority of cases, more than once.
2. Give them a few good reasons why they should use you for their travel purchases.
3. Allow the cards to fall where they may and follow-up when appropriate.

Not every sleep-deprived traveling marketing guy provided their credit card number at 3:30 a.m. just so they could be the proud owner of a bolt-sucking vacuum named after a fish. But I did. Marketing works folks ... but only if you give it a chance to work.

Here is what I want you to do. Get out and make it your business to connect with more people in your targeted audience. Tell them what you have to offer. Tell them what is in it for them. Some people will pay attention. Some people won't. And a few may even become your next client. (Stranger things have happened. I am proof of that.)

9. Respond To Leads Promptly

Here is a quote from a book I read titled **DO IT MARKETING** by David Newman. **"When it comes to responding to leads, the mantra is 'Now Or Never.' Leads won't wait. They are looking for a solution NOW."**

Regardless of the current condition of your business, leads are your key focal point when it comes to growing your business. Without leads you have no business-development plan. Without leads you become complacent and find yourself tending to your business as usual. Without leads you become lethargic and even boring. Yes, leads are the lifeblood of a growing business. **Generate more leads**.

Why is speed so important? Once a lead enters the picture, an imaginary timer begins a countdown. It becomes imperative that you respond to your lead in an expeditious fashion. Remember the window of opportunity does not remain open for long.

There are too many options available to consumers today. They have little time or patience trying to empathize with your lethargy. I have found through experience the first supplier to respond to a lead has a definite leg-up on the competition. Speed wins. **Be the first to respond.**

The reason you are contacted in the first place is because the prospect feels you are in position to help them. You are just one of many qualified options they can call. You need to recognize this "gift" and take advantage of this fleeting sign of interest and respond accordingly... with alacrity. (Speed)

In most cases the lead is seeking immediate gratification. They are reaching out for information and chances are their lack of patience will dictate their actions. The simple fact that you responded to them quickly is a clear sign that they are important to you. Among dozens of other things, people (you and me) like to feel important.

Leads won't wait for you. They cool with time. You do not have to allow this to happen. Remember the mantra cited above: **"Now or never."**

10. TGIT: Thank Goodness It's Today!

Tonight, I am going to take a little poetic license and do something I have never done in my column.

Everybody knows what the letters TGIF stand for so I won't insult you with an explanation. For many years my four-letter reminder is **TGIT**. These four letters stand for **Thank Goodness Its Today.** Waiting to celebrate on a singular day called **Friday** is a losing strategy. *There I said it.*

The word Friday is just another way to identify one of seven precious weekly time periods we have in each of our fleeting lives. Time waits for nobody, and "today" is the day we have been waiting for. And tomorrow will soon be another today. *Make it count.*

I want to direct you to a project I am working on with Travel Research Online. It involves **Podcasting**. This is an audio format for sharing useful information with people who are receptive to new ideas, tactics, strategies and experiences. Mine is titled **Mike'd Up Marchev** and is now listed on Spotify, iTunes, Google Podcasts, Travmarketmedia and soon to be other outlets. Take a peak and let me know what you think. Your creativity is bound to become stimulated.

https://www.travmarketmedia.com/author/mikemarchev/

The following falls under the topic of Market Research. I have been writing a daily column for nearly five years. Now that I think of it, I might be the original recipient of the affectionate title of "Wind Bag." (I digress.) If you are reading this book right now (and you are reading this chapter right now) send me a quick, short, painless email so I know somebody out there is reading my "stuff." mike@mikemarchev.com

You would be surprised how much a little input means to people. Let's expand on this thought. Starting tomorrow, if you are really serious about building your business, respond to those in your universe who are capturing your attention. Applaud their efforts and when appropriate, acknowledge their contributions to your life.

The sad truth is that very few people take the time to acknowledge superior behavior. The upside to this simple courtesy is ENORMOUS. (HUGE!)

Recap: (1) Take advantage of every single day. (2) Adopt **TGIT** as your new mantra. (3) Listen and subscribe to my new podcast. (4) Take time to professionally respond to people.

Today happens to be over. I hope you enjoyed every second of it.

(And tomorrow is another today.)

11. Sometimes Things Actually Do Work

My nephew and his girlfriend came to visit us this weekend from Brattleboro, VT. Andrew is my sister's son and we were looking forward to meeting his new friend.

The Marchev family consists of a large group of fun-loving people who spend a major portion of their time together laughing and kidding each other mercilessly. I am very pleased to report that Sarah impressed us and proved to be capable and willing to go "toe-to-toe" with us.

But that is not the theme of tonight's story. Andrew and Sarah met online. Yes. Through a dating App. Sometimes things actually do work.

If these two never rolled the dice, chances are they would have never found each other. They took a shot. It appears it was a winning shot. (The jury is still out.) I venture to say, although I have no direct experience in this field, that most dating app acquaintances do not work.

How does this budding relationship relate to your business? I think the correlation is obvious. Borrowing a quote from the great Wayne Gretzky of NHL Hockey fame, **"You miss 100% of the shots you don't take."**

I am sure about one thing as it pertains to your business. If you don't take the appropriate steps in the right direction, not much good can come from your apathy. Perhaps it is time that you take a risk in favor of your future. Maybe you can step out of your comfort zone for a minute or two and try something totally out of character. Who knows? Your "shot in the dark" just might hit the net. Someone once reminded us that even a blind squirrel finds a nut now and then.

Andrew found Sarah on a whim. Sarah found Andrew because she rolled the dice.

Sometimes things do work.

In the interest of time, I chose not to bore you with a few of my successes that came about as a result of my taking a chance. My many failures would probably prove more entertaining, but I will leave those for another day. As for now, let it suffice to say, tomorrow is another day. It is another perfect day to **"Go roll the bones."**

"Go roll the bones" = Roll the dice.

12. Stop. Think. Observe. Act.

This is perhaps the sagest advice I could give you as another day ends with hope for a better tomorrow. I am borrowing this title from another three-word reminder we are all familiar with when it comes to railroad crossings: *STOP-LOOK-LISTEN*.

Every 24-hours, when I find myself preparing for another night of restless sleep, I reflect on how time is passing without my permission. I am not sure where the finish line is or when I will be crossing it, but I do know I have a finite number of yards/miles to cover before my race is over.

What better time than tonight to remind you that lamenting about today's mistakes or down-and-out failures is not the most prudent way to spend the precious minutes before falling off to sleep. And as Fleetwood Mac sings so eloquently in song, **"Don't stop thinking about tomorrow. Don't stop. It will soon be here."**

Another tomorrow will soon be here. Put the Dow Jones, Covid-19, our personal political opinions, and the opinions of others aside for a moment.

STOP. Simon and Garfunkel said it best when they reminded us to, "Slow down. You're moving too fast. You've got to make the morning last." Smell the roses. Notice the cloud formation. Actually, taste your food tomorrow. Take a walk. Call a friend. Live in the moment.

THINK. How can you add meaningful value to the lives of others? What can you do tomorrow that will make a few of your close friends, associates and clients glad they know you?

OBSERVE. Pay attention to your actions tomorrow and how you spend your day. Notice what you are doing that works and what seems to be holding you back. Identify the pros and cons in your life. Make a decision. That decision is entirely up to you.

ACT. Review tomorrow's "To-Do List" and take a step forward. If you are not sure what to do, so something. Your actions will be responsible for your future results. Act.

I wonder! "Will your tomorrow be better than your today based on today's four-word action plan? **STOP - THINK – OBSERVE – ACT.**

*****Based on my observations and years of experience, I am afraid that most of your tomorrows will unfold exactly like most of your yesterdays. *Please prove me wrong*.

13. It Isn't Over Until It Is Over

I believe we give credit to the Yankee catcher Yogi Berra for this pivotal reminder. "It ain't over until it is over." An off shoot of this sometimes refers to an over-weight soprano singing the lyrics to God Bless America. ("It isn't over until the fat lady sings.")

According to the latest news reports summer is now over since Labor Day has come and gone. And although many people are beginning to act like Covid-19 is over, even without an advanced medical degree I can assure you that it isn't. But there is something more important than both of these examples that is not over yet. YOU.

You are not over yet. You are not done yet building, pursuing, enjoying, creating, caring, loving, crying, laughing and living.

The sad truth is that many people today are walking around like it is over for them. It appears they have "given up the ghost" and are just meandering through the rest of their years.

SNAP OUT OF IT. (As Cher succinctly pointed out to Nicholas Cage in the movie Moonstruck.)

At the expense of sounding like a broken record I will gently remind you that there is a lot more work to be done. By both you and me. Let the naysayers do their thing. Let the macho group swim against the tide. Let the "suits" drag their feet. Not you. Not me.

There are people out there who need us (Not everybody.) You are not "over" yet and the fat lady has not even started to sing. (Kate Smith)

Nobody can deny the fact that the past few months have not been challenging. I'm not downplaying this tragic 12-month period. Not for a moment. But our role in this tragedy is an ongoing saga. It isn't time to quit. It isn't time to stop moving forward. It idsn't time to stop living.

It isn't over until it is over.

And if you want to get philosophical, tomorrow is just about to begin again.

14. Your Tone Speaks Volumes

Someone once told me that elephants don't bite. Mosquitoes do. This is a clever way of reminding us that it is the little things that annoy us the most.

I was reminded of this when a former business acquaintance "reached out" and gave me an unexpected phone call. It had been a while since we last spoke which was a result of two busy people trying to make ends meet. It was good to hear his voice again.

In a few short minutes I detected uneasiness in his voice. I did not mention it at first as we were too busy catching up. Detecting a momentary break in the flow of the conversation, I couldn't help myself. I asked him point blank what was bothering him since his tone was a dead giveaway that something wasn't right.

He responded as one would predict, "Nothing's wrong. Why do you ask?"

"It sounds like you have 400 pounds of dead weight on your shoulders" I said. "Are you sure you're okay?"

I'll leave the story there for now. Hopefully, my point has been made. When calling people on the phone, the only thing you have going for you is your voice. Since I can't see you or interpret your body language, I must rely on your word choice, tone and inflection to fully interpret your message. Your voice has to carry the load. And although there might have been nothing wrong with my business friend, this man's voice painted a totally different picture.

The issue was that my attention drifted from his message to my apparently false interpretation. This is how it works. And this is what you must try to avoid. It is in your best interest to come across on all phone communications as the upbeat, happening person you are. You can't allow a little laziness to sabotage your business relationships. Your clients have too many other options for buying travel once they interpret you as somebody who is not absolutely delighted to be speaking with them.

We all have our personal issues, problems and concerns. I am fully involved with mine and quite frankly, I don't have the time or the interest in adopting yours as my own.

As a general rule, people like to be around people who are "upbeat and positive." With this in mind, here are my suggestions:

1. Be cognizant of your "tone" when speaking. What you are thinking may not be what others are hearing.

2. When feeling a little funky, stay off the phone. (If you do answer it, you better be good at pretending that you are feeling good.) It does not take much to destroy the goodwill you have been building for years.

3. Remember that 100% of your marketing dollars are spent for the single purpose of having someone contact you. When your phone rings, don't jeopardize your future by sounding like you are carrying the weight of the world on your shoulders.

Tone is an essential element in the marketing mix. Make sure that your tone is working for you and not against you.

15. You Market For Tomorrow

The following is not an isolated case. Your business is running along like a fine Swiss watch when out of the blue comes some unexpected input that sets you back on your heels. It could be a mechanical failure, a force of nature, a change in personnel or a runaway virus. Regardless of the source, your wheels of progress were just derailed.

I was introduced to an unfortunate situation earlier today and the solution, albeit a tad too late, was obvious. The company in question had been riding favorable winds when all of a sudden it became apparent that they would soon be in for some tough sledding.

Yesterday there was no need to market their services as their plates were full and the future looked rosy. Today however, a lack of business caused a great deal of stress with knee-jerk ideas of how to calm the storm.

When your back is to the wall the chances of a short-term favorable outcome are slim at best. Introductions take time. Relationships take time. Business takes time. As the old saying goes, "the best time to grow a tree was twenty years ago." The best time to safeguard your future was weeks, months and years ago.

Marketing can be thought of as "setting the table." And as we all know, setting a table comes long before sitting down and enjoying the meal. So, without exploring the many options of positioning yourself in your personal marketplace, I will leave you with the following thought:

Regardless of your current workflow and demands for your services, it will serve you well if you continue spreading the good word while remaining visible within your designated marketplace. Avoid stop and go marketing practices. Stay consistent. Be persistent.

Today will soon become yesterday's chapter. Tomorrow is a good night's sleep away. **Marketing is for tomorrow.** The time to sell will arrive soon enough.

16. You Didn't Get This Far By Accident!

You did not get this far by some quirk of fate. Granted, today's challenges may be unprecedented, but challenges of any shape and size are not new. We have come a long way since our first birthday, and we have always managed to overcome what seemed at the time to be insurmountable obstacles. Tomorrow is no different. You shall prevail.

I suppose tonight's message can be summed up by reminding you that

"What doesn't kill you makes you stronger."

The travel industry does not corner the market on this statement, as we both know that *plenty of stuff happens in our business,* and some *stuff* can be filed in the *"Why Me?"* folder.

Some stuff is down-right devastating, while other stuff just slides off your back. Some stuff stings while other stuff makes you laugh and scratch your head in amusement. **Bottom line: Stuff happens**.

Nobody ever implied that life would or should be fair. Nobody said that your business is going to be hassle-free simply because you are one of the good guys. In fact, that is *why* you are in business... to help your clients get over, through and around the rough spots.

Nobody is as good as you are when it comes to the phrase **"When the going gets tough, the tough get going."**

If booking detailed travel itineraries was easy there would be no need for you, your contacts, your experience, or your professionalism. You did not get this far in life by accident. Who you are today is the sum total of everything you have experienced along the way...both good and bad.

The result? You're okay. You are better than okay. You are good. You are *very* good.

Now get some rest because tomorrow you need to go out there again and be very good.

17. The Importance of Leading a Disciplined Life

"**Success is about doing the right thing, not about doing everything right. The secret to success is to choose the right habit and bring just enough discipline to establish it.**"

This quote is from Gary Keller and it is shared in his book titled *The One Thing*.

For years I have been asked to share my thoughts on **Time Management**. It is a popular theme and one that would draw huge crowds to a seminar room. Unfortunately, I am not qualified to offer any salient points on this subject. Reason being is that "time" does not require management. **YOU DO.**

The plight of today's travel advisor is the feeling they have to do everything themselves. Heaven knows there is not a shortage of "to-do's." The truth of the matter is there isn't enough time in a day to get it all done. There is too much to do and not enough time to do it.

This has the earmarks of a true conundrum. But the sad fact is you have all the time there is, and you can't possibly do it all yourself... nor do you *have* to.

Back in 1896 The Pareto Principle came to light. It reminded us that 80% of our results come from 20% of our efforts. Inversely, this implies that much of our time is wasted on tasks of little or no significance. I have a solution, and you can be sure it is easier to read than to implement.

In order to W.I.N. you must determine **What's Important Now**. That is the premise of Mr. Keller's book. On every to-do list, regardless of the number of tasks listed, there is just one item that represents "*THE*" one thing.

I realize that it would be easy to address tasks 1, 3, 6, 12, and 22 on your list of things to do and cross off all five thinking you are one efficient time machine. You would feel that you have this time management thing down to a science. That would really make you feel like you are "cooking with gas."

Regardless of the length of your list however, there is always a single entry (the "one thing") that deserves (and requires) your focused attention. The key is to concentrate on that "one thing" until it is completed to your satisfaction or you arrive at a logical stopping point. Only then is it time to turn your attention to the next "one thing."

It takes discipline to switch from quantity to quality. Starting tomorrow identify your "one thing" on your list and you will soon see that discipline will take care of your time management.

18. Take Responsibility For Your Future.

Author David McNally went on record to say, **"It seems there is no tougher challenge than to accept personal responsibility for not only what we are, but also what we can be."**

When I read this quote, I immediately remembered another line from the movie producer Woody Allen. The Woodster said he **"had accomplished many fine things in his life, but he managed to come up short on a number of occasions. What he did not accomplish was nobody's fault but his own."**

I have been sharing this quote with audiences for nearly 30 years. It is what I refer to as a **"Keeper."** Mr. Allen was given numerous opportunities to do more with his life, but according to him, he can't blame his failures on anybody but himself.

And so it is with your business. Since you do not have to place a large investment in inventory or raw materials, you have the ideal business model to succeed. You have equal access to the planes, ships, hotels, and destinations that are available to everyone. You have equal access to a market approaching 8 billion people and access to the required technology.

To accomplish your wildest dreams, all you need to do is decide if you are willing to pay the price in time and effort to (1) become visible and (2) to introduce your service to a handful of those 7 plus billion people.

If for some reason you do not succeed to the level you had in mind, chances are it is nobody's fault but your own. Let's net this out:

    Fact: You are who you are.

    Fact: You can be what you want to become.

    Fact: You must decide to pay the price.

    Fact: The ball is in your court.

Tomorrow is another day to accomplish what you don't want to regret in the near future.

19. Multitasking Is a Game For Clowns

"Clowns" may be too strong a word, but if it caught your attention I might as well stick with it. There probably is a milder word, but the subject of today's article is **"multitasking."**

In a previous story" I quoted author Gary Keller with a reference to his book titled **The One Thing**. Today I want to share a second quote from the same author.

"With research overwhelmingly clear, it seems insane that – knowing how multitasking leads to mistakes, poor choices, and stress – we attempt it anyway."

This topic has more flammability than a recent presidential debate. People in the travel industry (and in all industries for that matter) feel incredibly overwhelmed. They feel a necessity to keep a number of "balls in the air." My advice is to leave the juggling to the circus clowns. They get paid to juggle with no downside if they fail.

I have heard all your excuses and all ten thousand reasons why working on multiple assignments comes with the territory. Not unlike everybody else in this business you have lots on your plate and lots more riding on your effectiveness. You also can go excuse for excuse with the best of them.

That being said, I maintain my stance that the only person who benefits from multiple activity proceedings is ... nobody.

My personal definition of multitasking is **"the ability to screw up a number of jobs all at the same time."** Nobody wins. Numerous people become upset. You take one more step toward the Looney-Bin, and worse yet, you risk losing your credibility and the confidence of your valued clients as your work resembles mediocrity.

"Focus" is the word of the day, week, month and year. Focus is what it takes to avoid mistakes. Focus leads to making good choices while minimizing your debilitating stress quotient.

My advice to you is to leave the practice of multitasking to the amateurs. Take one focused step at a time. Work on one itinerary at a time. Slow down. Do the right things right. Become more efficient. Make more money. Stay in business. Smile more. Be happy.

Tomorrow is another day. The ball will be back in your court.

PS: The truth is you can do more than one thing at once, like iron while listening to the radio. But what you can't do is focus on more than one thing at a time. I rest my case.

20. A Gentle "Wake Up Call" Might Be In Order

Regardless of how many years you have been in business and how experienced you may be, a periodic **"Wake up Call"** is sure to come your way. And it just may be exactly what you need. My most recent "wake-up call" came last week as I was asked to edit a client's Special Lead Generating Report.

The piece was excellently written. Other than a few grammatical errors my contributions were incidental. That was not the "call" I am talking about. It came soon after the travel advisor shared his marketing strategy with me that I once again, "saw the light."

Here is tonight's bedtime thought.

The agent in this story is measurably successful by anyone's definition. He sells both high- and low-ticket items and has an envious referral record. In short, his business is humming along nicely.

But this seasoned professional understands how the game of business works. Today's good news is more often than not the result of a whole bunch of smart work performed in days past. One must continue "seeding and fertilizing" if tomorrow's crop is going to be worth harvesting.

But in his case, he was wise enough to know that "a bird in the hand is worth two in the bush." Although he was writing a lead generating special report, he did not want to take any of his current clients for granted. He understood what "first things first" actually meant. He had to solidify the current relationships he had with all his clients before setting out to acquire a new batch of customers. **And here comes the "wake-up call."**

His plan of action was to grab the attention and initial interest of just five to seven new prospects a month. This would leave him enough time to care for his current clients and still find time to follow up with his new batch of clients. Of those people indicating an interest in his special report, he would try to turn two into paying clients. In review: One Special Report – Five people raising their hand – two new clients.

BRILLIANT! This is very manageable. This is very realistic. This is very logical. This is very doable. This is very profitable.

The lesson tonight is two-fold. #1. Take care of your current customer list first. #2. Create a future lead generating plan that can be implemented day in and day out without you having to remortgage your house or give yourself a mild case of agita.

Before: Take care of your current client list.

After: Implement a slow, manageable lead generation campaign.

21. Clarity of Intention

"Clarity of intention launched with enthusiasm is the most potent combination known to humankind. It is the basis of all accomplishment." Author Unknown

Wanting to grow your business is admirable. Wishing for more profitable sales is a worthwhile objective. Hoping things work out for you in the long run should come as no surprise. Praying for the strength to do what is right also makes a lot of sense.

Wanting, wishing, hoping and praying won't do it. The hard truth is that you must do something if you want to see progress. But doing just anything is not the answer either. Although doing anything might be better than doing nothing, it will prove to be time ill-spent if you do not do the right things right.

If you are one of the many who still believe that sales is a numbers game you may be in for some hard times. Tossing enough "stuff" against a wall may result in some sticking, but it definitely is not the shortest or surest route to a larger bank account.

As soon as you see the light and compare the art of selling to a "game of darts" you will begin to add some girth to your bank account. (Reread chapter 5, page 14.)

Clarity of intention when speaking of sales implies that you have an unwavering idea (picture) of your targeted prospect. You know who they are by name and exactly what their needs are. You know what they look like, sound like, think like and you know the actions needing to be taken to stimulate meaningful forward progress.

Then with thanks going to your self-esteem and personal confidence quotient, you can show your selected audience how exciting the wonderful world of travel can be, and how you can help them enjoy the ride.

Your success will not arrive by accident. It will be directly proportional with your *clarity of intention*.

22. Are You Doing Enough "Laughing & Scratching?"

I was speaking with my brother the other day and he asked me if I ever began laughing out loud while driving down the road thinking how lucky we are? I said I knew exactly what he was talking about. As far as I am concerned, COVID or no COVID, political embarrassment or not, overall, I am generally pleased with my life.

For the first sixty years, I spent "laughing and scratching" down the road based on the mantra, **"Good enough is good enough."** At age 62 and for the next ten years I began questioning this philosophy. Looking back over my life I started to think that maybe I should have spent a little more time pursuing excellence. Perhaps if I did, I would still be "laughing and scratching" .... but on a higher level.

Then I read this passage and I began to ease off the accelerator.

> "Perfectionism is a self-protective mechanism that prevents us from flourishing through our vulnerability. It is particularly pervasive in professional contexts. Perfectionism isn't the pursuit of excellence, nor is it about self-improvement. It's really about attempting to win approval, where one's sense of self-worth is reliant on external measures of success. The sooner we let it go, the sooner we can start finding the courage to succeed and lead on our own terms."

Maybe being good enough is good enough. I know "good enough" could have been a little better at times. But maybe you just need to lighten up and spend a little more time just being you.

I've said this before. In all likelihood, you did not get this far by accident. Today, tomorrow and for the rest of the year, keep doing what you are doing with your own personal flair. If nothing else, you just might find yourself "laughing and scratching" until you too break into laughter while driving down the road reflecting on just how happy you are being you.

PS. Find more reasons to laugh...and perhaps a few less reasons to scratch.

23. Stop Worrying And Hit The Ball

It seems like just yesterday when I found myself browsing through my TV channels when I arrived at The US Open Golf Tournament. I remember saying to myself, "It is a shame there are no spectators," I watched an unknown golfer putt his ball and watch it travel 28 feet before disappearing into the cup.

My mind shot back to a book I read by Bob Rotella titled **"Putting Out of Your Mind."** I flashed back to a passage that read, **"Your problem is that you're worrying about speed instead of putting to make it."**

Let's think about this.

The golf ball is not moving. It is still and it is right in front of you. The hole is off in the distance, but you can see it from where you are standing. All you have to do is take aim at the hole and strike the ball in the direction of the target with the stick you are holding. How hard can it be?

But it is not that easy. Your mind clicks in and all sorts of information begins to fly through your head like a run-away horse and carriage. "Do this. Remember that. Not too far left. Not too hard. How is my stance? My grip? Should I wear a glove or not? What kind of grass is this? Am I detecting a slight fall-off toward the river? If I miss can I keep the ball below the hole." Blah... blah... blah. This is often referred to as mindless chatter.

Message: Stop worrying. There are only two types of putt: Putts that drop in the hole with a clunk, and putts that don't. What are you waiting for? Take a read. Make a decision. Hit the ball and you will find out soon enough which type of putt you will be experiencing.

I'll say it again. Do the appropriate diligence, do your homework, analyze the options and then "pull the trigger." I am sort of implying that you adopt the philosophy, "READY – FIRE – AIM. (But with a modicum of preparation.)

Okay! You have read tonight's message. Now tomorrow get up, get out, and make more people glad they know you.

24. A Lesson From Your Morning Crossword Puzzle

Something has been on my mind for days and tonight is the night I am going to get it off my chest. It involves the connection between a daily crossword puzzle and running a successful travel business. (Yes, as we age the mind works in funny ways.)

A few years back I was introduced to the online version of USA Today's Crossword Puzzle. It is the same one that appears in the daily paper edition. This was a new experience for me and in the beginning I found it very difficult to arrive at the correct solution for each clue. As a result, I opted for the "regular" version that notifies me immediately if I am making a mistake with red lettering.

I have noticed a few interesting occurrences over the years as I muddle through the clues. I will read a clue and have absolutely no idea of the answer. I will turn to another clue and immediately know the correct answer. The first letter of my correct answer was all that I needed to steer my thinking in the right direction to figure out the answer of the clue I previously had no answer for. (Did you follow that line of thinking?)

Sometimes I need two letters to solve the temporary conundrum. And on I go each and every morning, letter-by-letter, word-by-word until I smile with satisfaction knowing that I single-handedly accomplished another formidable "life-changing" task.

And so it is with our businesses. We often are presented with challenges that tax our knowledge and creativity. We appear lost until we receive a single clue in the form of some additional information. Then as if by magic, we arrive at the correct solution and life goes on as planned.

When you hit a roadblock in your business, think of it as an unknown puzzle clue. Don't quit. Investigate other clues that are more familiar to you. I am betting that the link (or chain) will soon become obvious and before you know it, you will be back on top of your game.

I realize today's story might appear a bit out in "left field" to you, but it made perfect sense to me.

Tomorrow, look for the clues that will lead you to more solutions. When you find yourself totally stumped, move onto the next project, challenge or next step in the process. More often than not, as if by magic, you will find yourself arriving at the correct answer.

25. Read *That* Book Again

It dawned on me recently that a well-accepted objective is to finish the book you start. More often than not, or primary mission is to get to the end of the book. When you stop to think about it this behavior is counterproductive. Let me see if I can explain my position.

You buy a book, or you are told to read one in school. The first thing you do is turn to the Table of Contents to see what lies in store for you. You might also flip to the back to see what kind of investment you are about to make timewise as you see this baby has 465 pages of ink. To make matters worse, the font is Times Roman in 10-point type. Yuk!

You begin your journey and you soon find yourself seeking logical stopping points. For many this is at a chapter's conclusion. For others it is on any page that ends with a period.

You are making good progress. You are already on page 137 and you are either heavily engrossed in the plot by now or you have learned a few new skills. You have only 228 pages to go. "I can knock this baby off in no time" you say to yourself as you turn off the light and adjust your pillow.

On the other hand, doesn't it make sense to slow your reading down in order to grasp each nuance as it appears in print? Picture the passing scenery and envision the budding relationship in the making. Stop worrying about "finishing" and spend more time comprehending and retaining important concepts. Who cares if you only manage to digest 5-6 pages per sitting? Your goal is not to "finish." Your goal is to think, concentrate, focus, interpret, analyze, digest, recall and learn.

Here is a novel idea. If you find a book you thoroughly enjoyed reading, (fact or fiction) read it a second time. The messages and enjoyment received the second time around will be just as exciting ... if not more so. As you grow as an individual, your interpretations change to fit your current surroundings. Read it again.

Tonight's message: Don't read for speed. Read to comprehend while expanding your knowledge base.

Tomorrow night I will share my thoughts in Part 2. My example will be the crossword puzzle.

26. Books And Crossword Puzzles: Part 2

Last night I shared with you my feelings on trading speed reading for focused comprehension. Tonight, I will shift to another daily practice that in many cases results in wasted opportunity.

As you now know, I begin each day by filling out USA Today's Online Crossword Puzzle. It dawned on me the other day that I was wasting an opportunity to enhance my general knowledge base in an effort to "complete" the puzzle.

Let me explain.

There are many clues that result with instant recall. You understand the clue and you immediately know the word. There are other clues that have you flummoxed right from the giddy-up. You have absolutely no idea what the answer could be. But with the help of the first letter, or perhaps a letter or two within the answer, your mind shifts into gear and "voila," you solve the line item.

You continue finding that many answers are filled in by simply addressing other clues. This is where the missed opportunity presents itself. You find yourself striving to complete the puzzle of the day by hook or by crook. You don't bother to digest the fact that the name of the author in five-down was a new piece of information. (In many cases you really couldn't care less who wrote XYZ back in 1845.) But my point is valid. There is a bunch of new information presented each morning and without pausing long enough to internalize this input, your knowledge base will remain the same. You already know what you already know. The idea is to build upon your base of knowledge, little by little each and every morning by being introduced to new information.

Here is what I suggest. After completing the puzzle in your normal fashion, erase the entries and play it again. This time focus on each and every clue and think about each and every answer. Pause. Think. Internalize. When I do this, the second pass through usually takes just minutes to complete. But by doing so, I retain a whole bunch of new knowledge.

I realize I may be preaching to the puzzle choir today, but as in most of my stories, I find myself writing to me. And heaven forbid, if you happen to be wired like I am, tonight's story just might give you something to think about tomorrow morning.

27. Don't Stop Thinking About Tomorrow

I am not wearing my "feel-good" hat today thinking I could make the world a better place by putting "lipstick on a pig." We are all currently facing the most challenging times of our lives. Make no mistake about it. We have been, and will continue to be, in for some challenging times.

But that being said, this is the hand we have been dealt. Our only recourse is to play our cards accordingly. What other options do we have?

It comes as no surprise to see some people walking around looking as if they have just lost their best friend. (Mask or no mask.) These people are clearly communicating that life is, and will continue to be, an unfair experience. Daily existence is a total drag for them while life offers nothing in return for their "showing up." If you know one or more of these individuals (and I'm betting you do) let me remind you that trying to improve the future of anyone engaged in an exercise in self-pity is an exercise in futility. You just aren't that good ... or talented.

Don't think for a moment that it is your responsibility to get these people singing happy songs. (It isn't going to happen.) Your job is to get *your* thinking straight, in step and positive so that you can significantly contribute to those anticipating a productive existence.

Here is today's phrase that pays:

You can't change the world... but you can change *your* world.

Your job is to energize yourself while making certain you don't get confused for the walking dead. Once you take care of you, your actions will do the talking. People are attracted to those who are alive, energetic, upbeat and happy – who have ideas and exciting plans for life – and who have kind things to say about others.

I love the Fleetwood Mac song phrase that reminds us to, **"Don't stop thinking about tomorrow. Don't stop, it will soon be here. It will soon be here ... better than before."**

So, if you truly want to become the exception, pick a game... any game... and get into the game with both feet. Become a positive player. **Never stop thinking about tomorrow**.

Good night.

28. Elephants Don't Bite

In a "me-too-only-cheaper" competitive, environment, strict adherence to the details (the little things) will position you faster and more accurately than just about anything else.

Take these three facts...

- **Fact**: Customers are in the driver's seat.
- **Fact**: Customers have a number of options when preparing to make a purchase– and they know what they are.
- **Fact**: Your success has everything to do with how you manage the "little things."

It is true that it takes many months to find a new account but only one goof-up to lose one. It makes sense then to pay attention to the **details** when it comes to dealing with prospects and customers.

Solidify the relationship you have with your base of accounts by making them glad they have selected you as their travel professional. Since the smallest error, mistake, misinterpretation or oversight could blow your previous track record out of the water (and set your company back a couple of months) focus on every little task at hand. Dot those i's... cross those t's ... and think "details."

Each and every employee must pull his or her weight. "Each" is spelled **(E-V-E-R-Y-O- N-E)**. Avoid shooting yourself in the foot and losing what you already earned for some foolish reason, or as a result of opting for a shortcut.

Here is a reminder for you. **NEVER** take a valued customer for granted. Pay attention to them especially when they **DON'T** have anything on the books

Now is the time to prove your value and worth to your current client base. You can do this by simply doing what you say you will do... the right way ... each and every time. Overlooking or ignoring the little things will put some major hurt in your life and it does not have to happen.

It is usually not the big items that will hurt you. It is the little things. Said another way, **Elephants don't bite. Mosquitoes do**.

See you tomorrow.

29. Failure Is Not Something To Avoid

Mistakes are good things. They are not something you strive to make, but they are not something you want to shy away from. The word mistake is synonymous with the word failure and failing remains your fastest way to progress. There, I said it again.

Think back to when you first mounted your two-wheel ride. (Bike) You did not master the concept the first time you saddled up. Somebody, (probably one of your parents) urged you to continue pedaling after you skinned your knee once or twice trying to find your balance. (If at first you don't succeed, try, try again.)

Then one day as if by magic, you began to roll. From that day forward it became impossible to lose your balance. Riding your bike became second nature.

Learning to ride your bike was hard enough. Learning how to turn a profit in your business today is a more formidable challenge. But it is not as hard as you may be making it. All you need to do is initiate a proven formula, and then learn something new each time you screw something up.

"Don't be silly, Mike," I can hear many of you saying. "Our job is to succeed; not fail." I agree. But doesn't it make sense to succeed as fast as you can? By design? Of course it does. His where "failure" enters the picture.

The secret is to become experienced. And as hard as you wish, hope, and pray, experience does not come without a price. It is the result of a great deal of consistent, focused action directed toward a worthwhile objective.

And here is a bonus idea for you. Once you get your "ducks in a row" and understand the steps needed to be taken, your efforts will begin to take on a life of their own. You will find that you will be enjoying the learning process more since you won't be beating yourself up every time you come up short.

Here is an analogy. The hardest thing in sport according to me, is hitting a baseball traveling at 95 mph with a rotation causing it to change direction on its way to the plate. The very best in baseball fail to hit the ball safely seven out of ten times. A .300 batting percentage ranks among the league's best. I am just as quick to suggest that running a successful business today is just as difficult as winning the batting title.

Message: Continue to gain experience by making more mistakes. Keep swinging. Fail faster. Fail more often. Fail with a purpose, but always fail while keeping your eye on the "target." The hits will come. The sales will come. The joy will return.

30. I Love It When a Plan Comes Together

One of the many truths I have learned during my 72 years of dancing and scratching my way to this point in life is that everything has a flip side. I mean EVERYTHING. To give you just one example: "Haste makes waste," is a phrase we all can come to grips with. But soon we are reminded, "He who hesitates is lost." Total opposite message.

Recently I was confronted with a situation where I had to decide if the fall was a good time to plant a little grass, or should I wait until springtime. I Googled the quandary and was soon confronted with two opposing opinions. One response suggested spring was the ideal time to green-up your front yard while another endorsed the cooler autumn weather. This is what is known in the horticultural arena as a "real conundrum."

I decided to cast my fate to the wind and before I knew it I was preparing my designated plot with a mixture of topsoil and seasoned goat manure. The month was September and the first frost had come and gone.

I'm sharing this story with you for a couple of reasons. First, you will be inundated with opposing recommendations as you pursue a successful career. There never seems to be one correct answer. Pick one. As they teach us in golf, line up your putt, make a decision as to its projected roll, and hit the thing. If it does not drop into the hole, hit it again.

In my case, I Googled. I read and I made a decision. I tossed a billion seeds into the prepared ground.

(To tie this back to business: I researched. I made a plan. I did something.)

Stay with me. This will all make sense in a minute or two. I knew that a billion seeds would not result in a billion blades of grass. But regardless of the outcome I knew my efforts to this point would all be in vain if I did not follow through with some focused attention. A regular watering routine was now in order. I began to water daily only to see ... nothing happen. I kept on watering. Still nothing.

Then one day as if by magic I spotted something that appeared to be a single blade of grass. It was green and it stuck straight up in the air. After focusing for a minute my eye caught a second blade. Then a third. My plan was working. I was growing grass. My efforts were paying dividends. I was a horticultural genius. (Horticulturalist may be the wrong word. Maybe Landscaper Extraordinaire paints a more accurate picture.) Whatever you call it, I was in my element.

Let me net this thing out in the interest of time so I can go outside and continue watering my budding lawn. (1) You must prepare the groundwork; (2) You must toss plenty of seeds knowing most will not germinate; (3) You must follow through and continue to manage your project; (4) You must keep on keeping on once you begin to see results.

As foolish as it may sound, I was genuinely excited when I saw my efforts paying noticeable dividends. My grass was actually taking root. I would have probably experienced the same results if I waited for the spring, but now I will be mowing my new project in May rather than still "thinking" about it.

Begin planting your seeds tomorrow and start watering them like your future depends on it.

31. You <u>Can't</u> Tell a Book By Its Cover

I woke earlier than usual this morning to stoke the fire, make some coffee and begin browsing through a few recorded TED videos. One of the more popular ones was only nine minutes long. Most TED videos are between 18-20 minutes in length. Short, sweet, and on point. I clicked on the nine-minute speech and was soon watching a young bathing suit model talking about self-image. (This woman was not the most polished speaker I have reviewed, but I immediately appreciated why this was one of the more popular TED videos.)

Although it would be highly entertaining, I won't bore you with the details of her presentation. I will, however, share the major take-away. This young lady was tall, slim and more than slightly attractive. Her message was that her success had a lot to do with her clothes, hair stylist, make-up artist, pre and postproduction professionals and more than a tad of re-touching of photos. She went on to say that although her highly polished appearance drew initial attention, nobody knew her for who she really was. She was a true to life example of the saying, ***"looks are not everything."***

She shared her observation that in the majority of cases "models" are lacking self-esteem and inner confidence. She reminded her audience that many (most) people spend the majority of their waking hours seeking an appearance beyond their current reality. Example: Taller; shorter; shinier hair; thicker hair; longer legs; slimmer waist; fuller lips; higher cheek bones, etc. They feel success lies in obtaining the "have-nots."

I personally interpreted her message as the importance of projecting the authentic you. Be who you are. Use what you have and know that even though you can alter your appearance, you will remain exactly who you are. And the people who count will appreciate you for who you are and not for what you look like.

I am not suggesting that you adopt a lazy, sloppy "what-you-see-is-what-you-get" attitude. A clean outward appearance with clothes that match more often than not won't do you any harm. A haircut now and then might also be in your best interest. Just don't go overboard spending too much time wondering, "why can't I be more like him/her?"

**** I know I have not done justice to this message. I can hear some of you saying, "That is easy for a model to say." Here is the link to the TED Video titled "Looks Are Not Everything" by Cameron Russell

https://www.youtube.com/watch?v=KM4Xe6Dlp0Y

32. The Next One Could Be The Big One

I was recently reviewing a few archived Inner Circle sales meetings and I came across the following soundbite: It was Thomas Edison who said, **"It is a shame to see many (if not most) people quit just one experiment short of finding the solution."**

This single sentence had my mind spinning with past phrases, suggestions, recommendations and reminders of mine with regard to the concept of quitting too soon.

One particular reminder came to mind. **"The next one could be the big one."** What does this mean? It implies that we do not know what the "next opportunity" will look like, sound like, smell like or taste like. We do not know if the "next one" will be the next phone call that will change our lives. Or the next email. Or the next introduction. Or the next sales letter. Or the next proposal. Or the next request for a referral. Or the next anything.

In baseball, the next pitch could be the one that meets the sweet spot of the bat and CRACK ... another run (or four) for the good guys.

Remember this: **"The next one could be the BIG one."**

I would be remiss if I did not remind you that 50% of all sales professionals quit after a single attempt at making a sale. An additional 25% stop calling on prospects after a second try. And here comes the differentiating statistic. 80% of all sales happen **AFTER** multiple contacts (Five or more.) If this does not put a little wind in your sales or some **"MOJO"** in your selling efforts than I must be speaking to deaf ears.

Bottom Line(s): (1) Don't quit too soon and (2) Keep swinging.

The next one could be the BIG one.

And if **100 bedtime stories** are not enough, I have some good news for you. My weekly column in Travel Research Online is waiting for you. "Mike's Monday Morning Cup of Mo-Jo." https://bit.ly/3tPfVUi

33. Podcasts "R" Us

Many agents have asked if I thought podcasts are a good way to remain visible. The answer is an unqualified yes.... with a "but" ... and a "however."

Like everything else you have at your fingertips, podcasts can prove to be a lot of work. They can also be a huge waste of time if you do not produce a meaningful broadcast with lots of good information. It helps if you find an audience who takes the time to listen to your words, opinions, experiences and recommendations.

The upsides are numerous

(1) You will become more knowledgeable as you research your upcoming topic.
(2) You will become a better presenter if you focus on your delivery.
(3) You will position yourself as a reliable resource.
(4) You will continue to build your relationship with your audience.
(5) You will have a tool which will help you gain access to hard-to-reach people.

The possible downsides.

(1) You don't prepare properly and come across as unorganized.
(2) You present "fluff" and fail to grab the ongoing attention of your audience.
(3) You fail to gain traction by not podcasting on a regular basis.

Producing a podcast and promoting a podcast are two different animals. There are many books and YouTube videos available to help you get started. For now, you might want to subscribe and listen to a handful of other topic-related podcasts to give you a feel for what is currently being produced.

Go to www.TravMarketMedia.com and in addition to my podcast titled **Mike'd Up Marchev** you can listen to a few more travel-related podcasts.

34. Simple Is Better

One of my favorite all-time magazine covers was a cover for Business Week. The year was 1996. Proctor & Gamble suggested that **we make marketing simple.**

"Marketers sell too much stuff in too many different ways. Now the smart ones are cutting the complexity."

Whoever said "what was old is new again" had their hand on the pulse. With more and more people becoming more and more familiar with the workings of the Internet, we are all being inundated with marketing come-ons from all corners of the globe. (I bet you didn't know the globe had corners. Either did I.)

Letting people know what we do, how we do it, and why we do it while positioning us as the "good guys" has become a daunting task. At times, it seems it is approaching downright impossible. Too many options. Too many people. Too much noise.

I've become oblivious to the **BOGO**'s offers. The **GUARANTEES**. The **FREE** initial consultations. **EXTENDED PAYMENT PLANS.** "**NO-RISK**" trial memberships. And the truth is that I have tried them all at one time or another with my marketing endeavors.

It is time we turn back the clock and take a hard look at P&G's Business Week Cover. What can you do to **MAKE IT SIMPLE?**

You can begin by being realistic. Understand your limitations and give a little more credit to your prospect's IQ. They know they have a plethora of options, and that you are not the only game in town. In many instances, they are more adept at working a computer and Googling for answers than you are. After all, they are FOCUSED on a single destination. Perhaps you would be better off seeing your clients as team members and not "target" audiences.

Next, you can give more than just lip-service to the notion that you can't be all things to all people. That was the error that P&G was focusing on. Take a bar of soap for example. There is no such thing anymore as a "bar of soap." Take a left down aisle five and you are confronted with no less than 200 choices of ways to wash your hands. (You don't believe me? Try buying some Tylenol. This exercise alone is enough to give you a headache.) Message: Make decision making easier. Narrow down your choices.

And finally, give your targeted audience what they are looking for and need most ... a person they can trust. Ask yourself, (1) Am I more interested in making a buck or in my client's total satisfaction? (2) Do I do what I say I'm going to do without exception or excuse?" (3) Do I try to make all relationships with me fun, easy and simple?

Twenty-four years ago, P&G put it on the cover. I think it is time we all get the message. **Simple is better.**

35. Some Ideas Are Worth Repeating

Let me rephrase today's title. Some **GOOD** ideas are worth repeating.

A few stories back I shared my views on how a daily crossword puzzle can effectively remind us of the concept of leveraging information appropriately. While I fumbled through the USA Crossword Puzzle earlier this week the lesson re-surfaced and I found myself smiling.

I don't say this very often, but this particular lesson is a "gem," and it is worth repeating. I will use slightly different words this time so as not to appear like a lazy slug by simply regurgitating my words from Story #24.

Same message. Different words. You read a clue sometimes and the answer immediately pops into mind. Twenty-two down, four letters. Clue: Popular shades of lipstick: REDS. Easy-peasy. At other times you read a clue and you literally do not have a clue. *Until you do.*

Six down. Six letters. Clue: Minor shortcoming. Nothing comes to mind. But once the four letters of six across are filled in and you see the first letter for six down is an "F" the word "**FOIBLE**" fits the bill. Voila! You cracked another one.

The same phenomenon is introduced in business on a daily basis. Some challenges resemble "a piece of cake," while others have us scratching our heads in bewilderment. When a clue pops into mind and we look at the current conundrum from a slightly different angle ... from a new perspective ...the answer becomes obvious. When the answer or solution enters the picture, you are once again off and running.

I apologize if today's repeated message causes any degree of consternation on your part. But some things are worth repeating. When you get "stuck" in a business-related situation, don't stop looking for clues that you are in position to address. Chances are the ball will continue to bounce and before you realize what happened, you will back in control whistling a happy tune.

Now before closing your eyes tonight you might want to flip back to Story #24 to solidify this message in your memory bank. Story #24. Page 34.

36. There's No Such Thing As "Down-Time"

I am often asked where I get my ideas from for my marketing columns. My answer: **EVERYWHERE**.

I remember a warm fall afternoon when I was cooling my heels in a Honda Dealership in Yorkville, NY. There are some things that just don't have to happen with a little planning.... and discipline. (1) You do not have to get a speeding ticket. (2) You do not have to run out of gas. (3) You do not have to own a car that does not operate as designed.

As a result, I service my car as the book suggests knowing I may be spending a tad more annually than needed. I just don't want to be bitten by #3 listed above.

Knowing what I do about car dealership reputations, I find myself lurking in a corner, masked up and paying attention to the service professionals as they pass through the sales department sharing a few lame jokes now and then. I have met many fine upstanding automotive professionals in my day, but by and large, I too approach them with a modicum of skepticism.

But that is not the topic of tonight's bedtime story. Utilizing "down-time" is what I want to address tonight. With time being our most precious commodity, it makes little sense to watch the secondhand sweep around the dial without our blessing. Yes, sometimes doing nothing is therapeutic and is exactly what the doctor ordered. (Sometimes.)

But with most of us dyed-in-wool entrepreneurs, down-time can be considered a blessing in disguise. Whether waiting for an oil change, a delayed flight to Chicago, a disturbingly late doctor keeping his appointment with you, or waiting for your significant other to aimlessly meander through the closest shopping mall, you have time to (1) review your latest proposal, (2) craft your next sales email, (3) draft an article you have been putting off, (4) return a phone call or two, (5) Google a series of potential group meeting locations, (6) delete outdated files from your laptop, (7) try your hand at USA Today's Crossword Puzzle, (8) outline the chapters of that book you have always wanted to publish ... and the list goes on.

With a modest dose of creativity, you too can eliminate the word "wasted time" from your vocabulary. Me? I am writing this reminder from the waiting room at Carbone Honda in Yorkville. I am planning to write five more before I check my blood pressure later today after seeing my bill for today's work. (I was putting off buying a new pair of "shoes" for "Old Betsy" so four new tires just may put me over the edge. I wonder if there will be a future article in there somewhere. Time will tell.)

37. The Path To Success Is Usually Less Traveled

Whether you are a Jeopardy fan or not, the following statement is as true as rain. The definition of an "easy" question is one that you know the answer to. It should come as no surprise then to hear the definition of a hard question. That's right. It is a question you do not know the answer to.

With this as the basis for tonight's story I would like to share a strategy I consider to be both "easy" and logical. It may be my 72 years talking coupled to my many years of accumulating more misses than hits, but I believe growing a profitable business is easy. I also believe that you are making it a lot harder than it has to be.

I do not see what all the fuss is about. Who said that building a business had to be difficult? Certainly not me. Like everything worth pursuing, it is the fundamentals that will get you to where you're wanting to go.

In an attempt to simplify tonight's story, I've outlined five steps that will have you feeling like a pro in very short order. The work stems from the concept of "consistency," and not from tedious and laborious "work."

Let's break this down to its component parts.

(1) Identify a market consisting of people who want what you have/do. This may be a hard pill to swallow, but current cruisers are more attractive than the larger group who has never donned an orange jacket in a mandatory lifeboat drill.

(2) Introduce yourself to this identified market. No buckshot approach here. Determine exactly who you need to get to know. You will target them and position them on your "marketing dartboard."

(3) Qualify this group to make certain that what you have is what will "scratch their itch." There is no future in trying to force a square peg into a round hole. Your time is best spent speaking with people who want to talk to you.

(4) Make yourself visible and available. Make it easy for them to contact you. It is your job to maintain both visibility and availability. When they do contact you, pretend that you are actually pleased they called. (You should not have to pretend. This should not be an exercise in make-believe.) And I should not have to say this ... but I did...and I do.

In time, you will be given an opportunity to strut your stuff... to showcase your expertise... to earn your stripes... to *cash their checks*.

That's it. That is all you need to do, every day, with consistency, with personality, and with a sense of professionalism.

But if this is so easy, why aren't more people successful at sales? That is also an easy question to answer. Because most people fail to buy-in to this formula. They feel that their gift-of-gab will deliver them to the promised land. Or they feel that if they build a better mousetrap, the market will find its way to their door. This is outdated thinking. This is mindless thinking. "How so, Mike?" you ask.

The entry-demands for selling travel are simple. You don't have to buy anything. All you need to do is to learn to say, "me-too" and go print yourself a business card with a multi-colored fancy travel-related logo. Add a clever saying next to some clipart and include your email address and VOILA .... you are a sales professional.

The options all consumers have today are limitless. At last count, there were 25 bazillion ways to book a trip to Europe or a room with an ocean-view in Cancun. The fastest way to the poor house is to do what everybody else does when it comes to selling travel. The fastest way to success is to adopt the formula I outlined above.

Here is an idea. Before crossing my formula off as another piece of marketing mumbo-jumbo, give it a shot. Adapt this formula to fit your own personality and see for yourself if it is a waste of time.

When can you start? How about tomorrow?

38. Nobody Owes You a Living

The last 12 months may not have won any awards, but we are watching the months come and go like never before. I heard from a local country "hay seed" yesterday that this year's colorful scenery was due to a lack of water. Sounded plausible to me. Color today. Bare branches tomorrow. "And the seasons they go round and round." Reference to a Joni Mitchell tune. (Circle Game)

Regardless of the month or the Zodiac sign we still have time to look for ways to build our businesses and continue to move forward with some semblance of positivity. And we can use every minute we have.

We have time to find and help more people begin planning their dreams while we introduce ourselves to more upbeat, fun, proactive folks out there in marketing land.

For many of you this is alarming news since you have been leaning on and blaming both summer and Covid-19 for the reason your business has taken a hit. Some agents felt it best to back-off during the midst of the Covid-19 Pandemic as a way to give their prospects some breathing room. I agree... kind of.

Among a few other things, I have come to learn that nobody owes me a living. And likewise, nobody owes you a living. What you do about your business is your business. But please, do not think for a moment that your competition is going to take the rest of the year off. Because some of them won't.

Please do not misinterpret my suggestion. I am not inferring that you become an arrogant, manipulative, sleazy, fast-talking, replication of yesterday's sales bag, or should I say "sleaze bag." Quite the contrary.

I want you to leap out of bed tomorrow morning with the intention of brightening up somebody's day. I once reminded you that a few choice words directed at the right person can indeed make a positive and uplifting impression. Never underestimate the power of your kind words.

What are you waiting for? Starting tomorrow morning get up and direct a few choice words toward your customers, prospects, ex-clients and preferred suppliers. Do what you can to bring a little sunshine to their world.

The operative word starting tomorrow is "**ACTION**." It really doesn't matter what you do as long as you do "something."

39. Don't Bite Off More Than You Can Chew

The following advice may sound elementary, mundane, or even amateurish to some of you. It isn't. Trying to do too much too soon is an exercise in futility. **Bottom Line:** Don't bite off more than you can chew.

I tell you this because in a few short months, you will once again be writing down the things you are not going to accomplish in the year ahead. Hence, my advice to you today is very timely.

With reference to your next to-do list, I have a better idea. I have a more realistic idea. I have a more logical idea. Why not write an "I plan to list" that has a genuine chance to work in your favor? Write down just **two** goals to work on.

For example:

1. Slowly build your current "good-guy" customer list by adding 12 more "good guys." For the sake of argument, "good guy" translates to "profitable." Just 12. One every four weeks.
   If you find yourself adding more names, don't panic. Just accept your good fortune.
2. Budget for some personal development. If you need a number, how does $250 sound? Now, you won't have to hesitate to buy a book, attend a course, join a webinar or subscribe to a personal development magazine. You can make Barnes & Noble your favorite coffee shop while they still exist. Since you have already budgeted for such luxurious expenses, it won't hurt at all. And there is no roll-over. If you don't spend this budget, you will lose it.

I know I said two, but here is a bonus item:

For the next two and a half months, work hard, honest and smart. The rest will fall into place, and you will find the days, weeks and months ahead will be kind to both you and your bank account.

I'm on a roll. Number four suggests that you "dump" five clients who are driving you nuts. The easiest way to do this without undue stress is to simply raise your management fee. Chances are they will eliminate themselves.

I'm going to skip a potential number five. But if I was forced to add a fifth, it would involve listing the ways you can have more fun. Starting tomorrow, start with #5.

40. Choose Your Words Wisely

This particular topic popped into my head early this morning for no apparent reason. I awoke to find myself thinking about words, phrases and sentences that were directed my way over the years.

You never know how your words may be taken by the recipient. For example, I don't think I will ever forget a particular sentence tossed my way by my college football coach back in 1968. I will spare you the specifics, but let it suffice to say, I have laid awake many nights reliving that particular brow beating.

Fast forwarding to the present I will try to shed some light on word choice by sharing a few more examples:

1. Saying "thank you" instead of simply saying "thanks" may appear as a little thing but in my mind conveys a vast difference in sincerity.
2. "Love ya" is a term used by many family members when terminating a phone call. "I love you" removes any doubt and delivers this heartfelt message clearly.
3. When responding to a "thank-you" from others, the term "No problem" in my mind is weak and lacking sincerity. A much better choice of words might sound like "You're welcome" or, "I am glad I could help."

You might think I am getting picky. I beg to differ. Your choice of words in any one particular instance can result in either moving closer or further away from developing a meaningful relationship with both prospects and current customers.

More often than not, a few more choice words will position you as the "real deal" and isn't that what you are looking to achieve?

On a different but in a similar vein, it is important to remember that not everyone has, or appreciates your sense of humor. I have been known to cross this line on more than one occasion only to be reminded by my wife.

I am not suggesting you put a tarp on your humor gene, but I am suggesting that you think twice before sharing that humorous one-liner that is aching to be released.

Thank you for reading tonight's bedtime story. I truly appreciate you spending a few moments with me. Tomorrow presents a brand-new opportunity to make a significant difference in your marketplace. Choose your words wisely.

41. Execution

E-X-E-C-U-T-I-O-N is a nine-letter word that has much to do with why most companies (and individuals) fail to meet their full potential. Said more accurately, it is the lack of execution.

According to Webster's New World College Dictionary –execute– is defined as: [to carry out; perform; do.]

The issue is not a lack of knowledge. It is a shortage of **"do."** Try this for the next seven days: Focus on the – **DO** – ...... the concept of execution.

Author Tom Peters (*In Search of Excellence*) once said: "It is amazing to me how many people in the oil business fail to get the message that in order to strike oil you have to dig a hole."

Popular clichés remind us that "talk is cheap" and "after all is said and done ... more is said than done."

If you want to strike oil dig a hole. If you want to grow your business, introduce your services to more people. (More of the **right** people.)

I'm not suggesting that planning, thinking, reflecting, and strategizing are not necessary steps in establishing excellence. I am reminding you that sooner or later you will need to put your money where your mouth is and put your knowledge, skills and personality into motion and **execute your plan**.

Here is a four-pronged strategy you can start tomorrow.

1. Finish what you start.
2. Concentrate on "barking up the right tree."
3. Perform every job-related task with the confidence of a professional.
4. Do what you say you will do.

Starting tomorrow, execute your skills with energy, enthusiasm and confidence.

***** When hit with a challenge, silently remind yourself, "I've got this."

42. Marketing Strategy # 7: The Interview

Tonight, I decided to feature one of my sixteen marketing strategies I share in my advanced training classes. I was prompted to do so after reading a SpeakerNetNews tip from Rebecca Morgan. The tip was titled... **The Interview**.

Do you remember Larry King? He was a slightly overweight man who sat on one side of a desk sporting a pair of fashionable suspenders and outdated eyeglasses. He would invite popular guests to his show to interview them. He asked questions without providing his opinion. His guests were the reason for tuning in.

Larry King was a well-recognized and respected TV personality and all he ever did was ask questions. In similar fashion, I could cite David Letterman, Johnny Carson, Jay Leno and today's Stephen Colbert ... all familiar names to some extent who prompt their guests to "share" experiences. Everybody who has trouble sleeping knows who they are.

In my programs I remind travel professionals they too can assume the role of interviewer. They too can become better known in their marketplace by simply inviting people to share their experiences and opinions with them. **The result:** You will become more visible while you build a reputation as someone who thoroughly knows the travel business.

Here is how this could work:

Step 1: You identify a reason for your interviews.

Your market is facing a challenge today. It is affecting your business like never before. It is called Covid-19. And you are interested in learning how it has altered your client's travel plans.

Step 2: Come up with a series of questions.

1. Have you had to cancel a trip in the last eight months? For what reason?
2. Are you planning to reschedule your trip?
3. Are you still hesitant to leave the safety of your home?
4. Do you feel the airlines have adequately safe-guarded future flights?
5. When will you feel it is safe to travel freely again?
6. Do you feel masks will become the norm when traveling?
7. Is your "bucket list" a thing of the past, or is there some destination you still dream about?

Step 3: You make a list of people to call.

Start with just three or four names so the task does not overwhelm you. You will soon add to this list as you find yourself actually enjoying these conversations ... while learning a great deal in the process.

Step 4: Make the call.

Call each person on your list and tell them you are writing an article involving current Travel Trends. You would love to hear their opinion on the subject. You then ask if you can "schedule" a better time to chat. Chances are they will be available to speak with you at that time, so be prepared with your list of questions.

Step 5: Take notes

This step is self-explanatory but make it clear how much you appreciate their input. Remember, you are not making a sales call. You are conducting a professional interview soliciting their candid thoughts on the subject.

If you maintain a friendly yet professional tone, chances are you will make a positive impression without appearing as hungry or pushy out for personal gain. Don't be surprised when the person you are speaking with begins to ask you how you run your business, and if you might be in position to assist them with their future travel plans.

I realize your mind is probably spinning with the names of many people who would be prime candidates for your interviews. Try to curb your enthusiasm... at least until tomorrow morning. It has been a long day. Try to get some sleep.

43. Lessons From A Fabric Store

You are probably wondering if Marchev has gone off the deep end? No I haven't. Not yet. I want to share an observation I once had in a fabric store of all places.

My wife Barbara and I were strolling through a fabric store looking for decorating ideas when the subject of tonight's story hit me.

After being in the store for just a few minutes I felt a mild migraine coming on, and I don't get migraines! I was being introduced to the Three C's. Choices, colors and the associated *cost*. I must admit there was a lot of good-looking "stuff" in that store. In fact, my eyes started to glaze over as the myriad of styles, fabrics and colors began to overwhelm me. Apparently, choices, options, and colors are all needed to sell tile, carpets and related gizmos. (I really don't get migraines, but you can picture my oncoming chagrin.)

Here was what caught my attention and stopped me in my tracks. On top of one of the counters was a one-foot square tile sample. It was a mosaic pattern if I had to give it a name. My wife was drawn straight to this "sample." The store manager mentioned that two people purchased this exact mosaic pattern the day before as a result of spotting it on the counter. They saw it – they liked it - they bought it. (My wife spotted it, but she wasn't ready to buy yet).

My advice to the store manager was to display what she wanted to sell. Car dealers have known this for years. Show room display cars sell *quickly*.

Vision is a strong selling feature. People buy what they can "see."

It helps if you can paint a picture. Any picture. A fun picture. Tell the story, *your* story, in *your* words, but in words that can paint a picture in the buyer's mind. Let people "see" what you are talking about. This particularly holds true with exciting and exotic travel destinations.

Toss in a little sincere enthusiasm and some good things are about to come your way.

Take it from me. Pictures sell.

44. Are You Climbing Up The Wrong Ladder?

If you have been reading any of my daily articles over the last four years, you know I have a penchant for the "analogy." *(Comparison; similarity; equivalence between independent parts; a form of reasoning.)*

Tonight's idea came to me while I was climbing to my roof to replace a few loose shingles torn by a recent windstorm.

You probably never stopped to focus on it, but ladders are potentially dangerous constructs. Notice how many "warning" labels are glued to the sides of your ladder. Just like Jim Croce recommended in song "not to mess around with Jim," I'm telling you not to mess around with ladders.

But ladders are both useful and in demand once you determine that your goal, or objective is slightly out of reach. You select a tool to help achieve your purpose. Enter: the ladder.

You lean the ladder up against a supporting wall and begin to climb. Step-by-step you position your foot on each rung, while always maintaining balance until you elevate yourself into a targeted position.

NOTE: I failed to mention that prior to ascending, (1) you take the time to check and double check ensuring the base of your ladder is firmly positioned and rock steady, and then (2) you have somebody help steady your ladder as you begin to climb.

"Mike, enough already. Shingles. Roof. Ladder. What's the message in tonight's story?"

You've got my ladder scenario firmly embedded in your head. I want you to picture the ladder as a means to an end. Most of you already have your ladder in place, and most of you are moving up in the right direction. But many of you might have your ladder positioned on the "wrong wall." You will soon get to the top, but it just might be the wrong top.

You may be climbing your own ladders hoping to achieve success. (In this case your ladder represents your marketing plans.) But there is also a good chance that you have placed your ladder against the wrong wall. You are busy ascending toward the wrong objective.

Let's net this out. (1) Select the **RIGHT** destination. Make sure you are pursuing your intended objective; (2) Choose the **RIGHT** tools, (ladder/marketing gambits) (3) Take each step one at a time while always maintaining your balance. (4) Be aware that any misstep could result in some serous discomfort. (5) Don't begin to climb until you are convinced you are on firm ground. (6) Don't multi-task while climbing your ladder. FOCUS. CONCENTRATE. PAY ATTENTION.

45. Repetition Is Not a Bad Thing

Tonight's message came to me the other day while I was trying to come up with a clever title for a new article.

I couldn't help but reflect on a recent article I wrote using the crossword puzzle as an analogy. It was "spot on." I wanted to share it again, but perhaps with a slightly different twist. Rather than sound like a broken record, I decided to come up with something "new."

That is when I took a break to sit down at the piano and played three songs I have been working on. I noticed I was playing each more fluidly while thinking less about my next chord change. My playing was sounding a lot more like music. How did that happen?

I realized that my musical improvement had everything to do with *repetition*.

If I haven't lost you by now, here is tonight's message: Practice. Never stop practicing. When you think you have something down pat, practice some more. I am reminded of a quote from an NFL Hall of Famer who played for the Los Angeles Rams, Merlin Olsen. The big guy once said, **"If I am not practicing and my competitor is, when we meet, they will beat me."**

I have been quoted as saying the difference between in amateur and a professional is amateurs do things when they want to. A professional does things when it is time to.

A professional never stops practicing. He or she recognizes the value of doing the right thing at the right time in the right order over and over again. And to pull this off consistently one must practice beyond boredom or fatigue. The term "muscle memory" comes to mind.

I have often been reminded while teaching graduate school students that I have adopted a nonlinear delivery style. I hope that you can follow my often-times bouncing train of thought.

One last point before you turn out the lights. Practice alone does not make perfect. Practice makes permanent. Practicing the right things makes perfect. **Good night.**

46. Are You Protecting Your Greatest Asset?

The latest audible book I am listening to is by Greg McKeown titled **Essentialism**. It is about understanding what is essential while discounting the rest. I listen to a chapter every night while lying in bed ready to call it a day.

When I heard the phrase, "Are you protecting your assets?" I sat up and made a note to myself immediately.

It has been said by many people: **YOU** are the product in a service organization. **YOU** are the true differentiating factor. **YOU** are the reason in a me-too industry people select you as their service advisor.

Advice from Navy Seals training reminds candidates, **"A dead man cannot save anybody."** This is a succinct way of reminding us that we must ensure that we are in a solid position and in good health if we are going to help anybody. **YOU** first.

Flight attendants remind us to secure our own oxygen masks before going to the aid of our children. This may sound selfish, but it is the prudent thing to do. The reasoning is exactly the same. **YOU** first, so you can help second.

If **YOU** are the differentiating feature of your company, that makes **YOU** a true asset. That means **YOU** must be worthy of protection.

It is high time that you start paying more attention to **you**, your strengths, your capabilities, your frame of mind and your never-ending opportunities to be of service to your targeted audience. Did I mention your health, your emotional intelligence and your sense of humor?

If you are not actively helping your clients, then it is time you continue to help yourself. This can be accomplished by (1) reading, writing, attending workshops, (2) watching supplier webinars while taking time to internalize your notes, (3) meeting with prospects and asking questions, (4) brainstorming with your peers, and (5) joining like-minded business-development groups. Little-by-little. Step-by-step. **You** first.

YOU are an asset. Make no mistake about it. **You** are worth protecting. Make no mistake about it. Recognize that you are a true asset to your clients. Make no mistake about that. Decide what needs doing to become a better **YOU**. Then starting tomorrow, begin improving and adding to your value. But for now, it is time to rest. Good night.

47. Don't "Throw In The Towel?" Not Yet!

Having always considered myself a realist, I have a few thoughts to share about "throwing in the towel." And make no mistake about it. The day is coming when those exact four words may very well appear as an attractive option. And yes. I have been known to utter these four words myself. (Shame on me.)

I fear the day when you are going to feel the full brunt of all your "useless" efforts. That's the day you will want to call it quits, and "throw in the towel." This will not be the action of a sore loser, but as a conscious decision from a hard-working, good intentioned entrepreneur who feels their efforts have all been for naught for the past twelve months.

The term "emotional intelligence" just flashed across my mind, but that is not what I want to talk about tonight. I also will avoid repeating what you have been hearing from a hundred other "know-it-alls" when all this doubt first entered your mind. In the interest of time, and in an attempt to protect my reputation for "shooting-from-the-hip," I will say what I came to say.

When the going gets tough, (and it really doesn't get any tougher than it is right now) there is not a man, woman or child alive today who will not entertain the decision to give up, cry uncle, turn the page, roll the dice in a new direction and quite simply, "throw in the towel." I would be less than honest if I said I have not tussled with this decision myself on a number of occasions the past few months. I often feel I am "spinning my wheels." I guess there is something to the statement, "We are all in this together."

For a few of you, if the truth be known, "throwing in the towel" would prove to be a wise decision. Many "travel advisors" joined our industry for the love of travel. They are not, have not, and will never pay the price for true service professionalism. The game board has been altered significantly, and I am afraid only the cream will rise to the top.... as it has been known to do.

But most of you provide a valuable service and will continue to do so when the pendulum starts swinging back through some semblance of "normal." I wish I could tell you when that will be. I can't.

I have no idea of your financial position, or your relationship with your clients and loved ones. What I do know is this:

1. Your homerun may be coming with the very next pitch. (A single, double or triple would also be welcome.)
2. What you are dealing with at the moment is not strictly confined to you.
3. You did not get this far in life by accident.
4. Brighter days lie ahead.

5. I think I know that throwing in the towel, although an alluring option at times, and perhaps one appearing more and more attractive, may not be the right move at this time.

I can't help believing that your clients are "chaffing at the bit" when it comes to cabin fever and the urge to get out of town again. Your career will soon begin to blossom. But in order to "blossom" you must be ready, willing and able to spring into action once the light turns green. Your job to educate your clients and help them make better travel-related decisions will once again be in demand…and very much valued.

My advice tonight? Hold on to that towel for just a little longer.

48. Three "Brilliant" Reminders

Get Ready For a Curve Ball. Here it comes.

In over four years of writing a daily column for Travel Research Online, I have never done what I am about to do. (Don't you just love the suspense.) Tonight I will be introducing you to something new.

No, I am not going to write this article while riding an elephant naked down Atlantic Avenue in Delray Beach, Florida. (I'm just wondering after reading that last sentence, are you envisioning a naked elephant, or an old guy with no clothes on? Just asking.

Instead, I am going to share three of my favorite quotes with you. Each one consists of a few words of wisdom that have me pausing and reflecting before moving on. This is a first. I hope you will find it to be as exciting and worthwhile as I do.

"If I am not practicing and my competitor is, when we meet, they will beat me."

Merlin Olsen, Former NFL Football Hall of Famer

Merlin hit the nail right on the head with this one. Practice, repetition, trial and error is the name of the game if you want to gain entry into your personal hall-of-fame. The good news is that most people do not, and will not, have the discipline to continue practicing when they feel it is time to stop practicing. You can follow the leaders in any endeavor, and you will see the same thing. The winners will be recognized for their discipline when it comes to practice.

"It is amazing to me how many people in the oil business fail to get the message, in order to strike oil you have to dig a hole."

Tom Peters, co-author of In Search of Excellence shared this poignant reminder. Most people talk about it, plan about it, think about it, dream about it, brainstorm about it, and do everything they can to avoid doing something about it. If you want to find oil, dig a hole. If by chance you hit an empty hole, dig another one.

I am not suggesting you approach any worthwhile program with wild abandonment or a lack of respect. I do endorse a certain degree of planning and thinking about your next move.

But to avoid insulting your intelligence, I will leave this message up to you. I will give you a hint. **Less talk – more action.**

One more ...
Howard Cosell once interviewed Jimmy "The Greek" Snyder. (A lawyer and a "bookie.")

When asked what he liked best in life, Jimmy quickly responded with, **"I like to win."** The follow up question was, "What do you like second best in life?" Just as quickly Jimmy responded with,

"That's easy Howard. I like to lose."

What "The Greek" was saying in no uncertain terms that day was **he lived for the action**. He knew he would sometimes win a bet. He also knew he would experience his share of losing. But it was "the action" that kept his juices flowing, and his mind in the game.

Are you too focused on winning …at all times …at all cost? Or, are you allowing "the action" to be your drug of choice?

I can hear some of you saying, "That is all very fine and good was Marchev, but I would have preferred the naked elephant scenario." I am hoping your dreams tonight do not include a naked man riding an elephant down Main Street. If so, please accept my apologies.

49. Some Good Advice For Job Seekers

If you have been reading my articles you probably find yourself disagreeing with me from time to time. If you find yourself disagreeing with me more often than not, I suggest you stop reading and go pursue the pastime of your choice. This is known as emotional intelligence.

But even if you do agree with my opinions now and then, I just may test your loyalty with tonight's story.

First of all, I am not a big fan of the job resume. That statement, in and of itself may sound sacrilegious to some of you. Remember, tonight's story is being written by a "maverick." I feel that the time spent crafting and editing a detailed document outlining your qualifications and how "really cool" you are is more or less a waste of time. I say this because your resume is literally one of hundreds that look and sound EXACTLY the same. In my opinion the resume is the ideal tool to make the selection process a whole lot easier for the decision maker by helping to disqualify candidates quickly and without much thought.

You must admit all resumes look alike and sound pathetically similar. The job seeker often forgets that although the reader may appear to be in a position of authority, they too feel they are over-worked and under-paid. Eliminating candidates is far easier than separating fact from fiction. Especially when the wrong selection could cost them their jobs.

If you are open to hearing a professional opinion that is reality-based and designed to capture the attention, as well as the imagination of the decision maker, I say, **lose the resume**.

In any sales situation, regardless of the service, product or industry, step one calls for capturing the buyer's attention. This won't happen if you insist on playing the same ole "pick me" resume game. You must step away from normal mob behavior and position yourself as "**someone special**" right from the get-go.

Here is what I suggest you do the next time you want to start work on Monday.

First, decide what gives your future supervisor (your boss) their biggest headache. Regardless of the industry or day of the week, I will now tell you exactly what that is.

   (1) They want an employee they can count on; one that will come to work ready to work every day ... on time ... with a semblance of a personality.
   (2) They want an employee who does not come with an attitude. They are looking for people who are "coachable" and who have a keen desire to improve.
   (3) They are looking for an employee who is willing to contribute and will professionally represent both the company and their boss. A sense of humor never hurts either.

Everything else can be taught in very short order.

Here is what I want you to write to your next potential employer:

My name is Mike Marchev. After researching XYZ's latest accomplishments and plans for the future, I have come to the realization that 1) I believe I can personally contribute to the growth or your organization, and 2) If given the opportunity to do so, you will not regret your decision. How can I say this?

> *(1) I will show up ready to work every day .... on time. (Everyday)*
> *(2) I am a team player and I am coachable and receptive to input.*
> *(3) I will perform my duties without exception and without excuse.*

How soon can I begin proving my worth to you?

And Then There Is Sales

To those who are not looking for a new job, this same strategy holds true when trying to sell a new client on your services. Refrain from waxing eloquent. Tell the prospect the four things you can provide as soon as your business-relationship begins.

Simple sells. Truth sells. Results sell.

50. Did Somebody Say "Attunement?"

This next quote was taken from the book **To Sell Is Human** by Daniel Pink.

"It is an excess of assertiveness and zeal that leads to contacting customers too frequently. Extroverts often stumble over themselves. They talk too much and listen too little... which can be read as pushy and drive people away."

For years it was believed that successful sales personnel exhibited an outgoing, people-oriented, fun, and vivacious personality. Sales pros had one thing in common, and that was the "gift-of-gab." They could mix and mingle with anybody at a moment's notice. (Keep this to yourself, but forty years ago I failed a test for a high-level sales job because I was not considered extroverted enough. Bummer!)

As consumers were given access to more information and became smarter as a result of their own research, less demand was placed on the extrovert of yesterday when it came to selling. In fact, today's successful sales professional might even border on the introverted side of life. They talk less and listen more. (It appears I was perhaps, ahead of my time.)

The pushy, aggressive, master of the "close" salesperson has fast become yesterday's news. Slowing down. Backing off. Asking more meaningful questions and taking the time to listen while internalizing the feedback is the key to more sales.

That's my message tonight. Slow down. Stop talking. Start listening. Begin selling. Go to sleep.

Tomorrow you can begin introducing the new you to your marketplace.

51. In Search Of That Elusive "One Thing"

One of my favorite movie clips came from the movie City Slickers. Billy Crystal was riding alongside the tough-guy cattle herder played by Jack Palance. (Curly) Curly said the secret to life was just **One Thing** as he held up his pointer finger. Crystal was all ears as that was exactly what he wanted to learn from the crusty old cowboy. "What's the one thing?" he asked. "That is what you have to find out," answered Curly, as he rode out of frame.

For many, the hope of finding the "one thing" will come in the form of a magic pill. There seems to be a pill for just about everything these days ... from headaches to pain to weight loss to cholesterol control ... to unforeseen "intimate moments" for you old guys. Yet most sales and marketing gurus, coaches and trainers are quick to remind you that there is no "magic pill" when it comes to business success.

There is not "one thing" that works for everybody. But you do have something at your beck-and-call that will work for you. It is not generic. It is your personal brand. And therein lies the rub. Just like Curly shared with Billy the city boy, you have to discover it for yourself. You have to find it. You have to polish it. You have to use it. You have to learn from it. You have to work at it.

Your "one thing" is different from mine. Mine is different from yours.

The "one thing" comes in different sizes, colors, shapes and styles. The single common denominator is that all "one things" usually fall under the umbrella known as **m-a-r-k-e-t-i-n-g**. They all involve getting the right people to know you, like you, and eventually trust you. Whichever "strategy" you choose to use, you must do so daily ... without exception ... without excuses ... or your "one thing" will soon become just "another thing."

"**One Things**" take the form of networking; emailing; written communications; public speaking; blogs; websites; demonstrations; home parties; proposals; contests; collaborations etc. Your "one thing" is no better than mine. It just is a better fit for your budget, time constraints and personality. And your "one thing" is the "one thing" that works for you. As long as you practice your "one thing" daily you have a good chance at enjoying the results.

As you prepare to call it another day, I challenge you to find, begin developing and refining your own **"One Thing."**

I also challenge you to do something that you may have been avoiding for the past ten months. Try with every fiber of your body to have more "***FUN***" in the months ahead. Now that sounds like "one thing" I can focus on.

52. From Annoying Pest To Welcome Guest

I recently received three emails from members of my Inner Circle Group asking me to critique their recent attempts of drafting sales letters.

In all three cases I spotted a common mistake as well as a few other errors which I felt compelled to comment on. Let's see if we all can learn something from my recent experience.

Because your topic probably is a subject you feel comfortable with there will be a tendency to write about your qualifications, sincerity and interest at the expense of the more important focal point. **THE READER**.

Here are a few of my suggestions. (If the shoe fits, wear it.) If I am not talking to you, stop reading and get back to brushing your teeth.

1. Decide whom you want to write to.
2. Determine what you think they **want** to hear.
3. Decide what you want them to do as a result of reading your letter.

Once you have a feel for the above three steps, begin jotting down possible answers. This simple exercise will help you focus on what is important. This task will soon take shape and become easier as you continue to *draft* your thoughts.

After completing your first draft, I want you to perform the following exercise. Count the number of times you refer to yourself vs them. I, my, we, us vs. you, yours, them, theirs.

Remember

1. Nothing positive can happen if your letter does not get read.
2. They will not read your letter if they don't feel there is something in it for them.
3. They don't give a hoot about you, or the horse you rode in on.
4. Assume, (and correctly so) your readers will be asking themselves these questions: a. What's in it for me? b. Why should I care? c. What's the upside of doing what you are asking me to do?

I don't believe there is an answer to the question: "How does one write a sales letter that works?" There are too many variables at any given point in time to hang your hat on just one hook. I am afraid I have to say what you do not want to hear. "**Trial and error.**"

Test your letters and see for yourself what works. Just hedge your bets by NOT shooting yourself in the foot by making common mistakes of self-interest.

I'll leave you tonight by sharing the salesman's mantra which encompasses both letter writing and in-person presentations: **BE BRIGHT; BE BRIEF; BE GONE.**

53. Follow Up Never Goes Out of Style

When I started thinking about retirement, Barbara and I began investigating log cabin homes. We did what any investigators might do ... purchase a log home magazine at the supermarket and send away for all the free stuff that was not nailed down. Send we did. Stuff we got.

But here is where tonight's lesson begins.

I am absolutely appalled at the lack of professionalism shown by the log home industry. Sure, they got an "A" for sending stuff just the way every other company gets an "A" for sending stuff from direct mail, trade shows, etc. This is the easy part.

But as the weeks passed and I had not received one phone call following up my clear sign of "interest," I began to think less of the industry.

Haven't log cabin salespeople ever been introduced to the Rule of 7? Didn't anybody tell them the importance of appearing a little interested in potential buyers? Don't they realize that I just might have a few other things to think about during the course of any given day and that I might appreciate a little attention from an expert home specialist?

I had no idea that log cabins were such in demand that all you need to do is shoot out a few catalogs and take orders.

The smart log cabin salespeople (by my definition) would spot a guy who raised his hand silently indicating:

"I'll bite. Teach me something."

They would then follow the catalog with an easy-to-read brochure or email explaining how a septic system works in the middle of the woods or how to dig a hole in your backyard and find water, or how to squeeze a little "juice" from an electric pole to a remote location ... or how to shoo bears off your back porch, or how to bake biscuits on a wood-burning stove and/or 1001 other trinkets of information that a rube from New Jersey might want to learn about prior to sticking himself, along with his family, on top of a hill in upstate New York.

Enough about me and my housing conundrum. What about you?

When you witness a potential client raising their hand, do you seize the opportunity by plugging them into a logical follow-up program? I certainly hope so. Because if you don't, these very same would-be clients might be bad-mouthing you as an uneducated professional who isn't motivated enough to play the game the way it is designed to be played. This is not the ideal situation.

I am not talking about becoming overly aggressive, pushy, arrogant or sleazy. I am inferring that you show a little interest and professionalism.

Remember:

1. When you are out of sight, you are out of mind.

***The Rule of 7 indicates that you must follow up more than once.

2. It is not their job to follow up. It is yours.

    ***The Rule of 7 reminds us that in order to do business with somebody who is not familiar with you or your service it usually takes a minimum of seven contacts in each 18-month period to gain traction in the relationship. The numbers I just cited may vary. The key point is that consistency and persistence will pay dividends moving forward.

54. What Does a Clogged Gutter Have To Do With Anything?

Have you noticed more commercials on television these days promoting the benefits of protecting your home from gutter leaks? You will now. I just called your attention to it.

What I find interesting about these advertisements is their focal point. It became clear to me almost immediately that they were not referencing how dried leaves backup in gutters and can clog the downspout. Water then builds up and backs up until it freezes. Then the fun begins. Ice creeps up the roof and soon, with the sun and the warmth coming from inside your home, the ice melts and finds its way into the under layers of your roof, and down into your ceiling. The damage resulting to your ceilings and walls can easily add up to thousands of dollars. Not much good results from clogged gutters.

These ads do not mention the damage ice can cause as a result of a backed-up gutter. There are not many products on the market today less sexy than gutter shields. A toilet plunger comes to mind, but let's not go there.

What the ads do shed light on and calls attention to is the dangers involved in climbing a ladder. They focus on the safety aspect of one's annual ascent to your roof's water trough. In addition to falling off an unstable ladder, it is not uncommon to cut your hand while scraping through the aluminum channel for soggy, decaying dead leaves, sharp twigs and all sorts of nasty debris.

What does this observation have to do with you? I see a lesson here hiding behind your gutter shield. Are you, or do you spend most of your limited "airtime" talking about the destination and means of getting there and back? Or, do you see the value in focusing on your prospect's underlying true interests?

Clearing a gutter or two once a year is no big deal. But schlepping a rickety ladder out of your garage, around to the back of your house, finding a pair of old work gloves, making sure the ladder is stable, picking a day that is not too cold or windy, and bagging the rotten, moldy, wormy decaying leaves so they can be picked up by your town's garbage collector on Wednesday sounds like work to me.

I hope you made the connection to ALL the work that goes into booking a vacation these days considering all the unknown variables and health/safety considerations.

You are not selling a destination. You are selling peace-of-mind. You are selling attention to detail. You are selling peace of mind knowing that everything which needs attention has been attended to. You are selling the notion that you are removing all forms of ladders and unknowns from the equation and paving the way for nothing but smooth sailing.

I don't want a gutter shield. I want to know I don't have to climb up on the roof again.

55. My Thoughts On Integrity Selling

"PEOPLE ARE MORE APT TO BELIEVE YOU WHEN THEY SEE A CONGRUENCE BETWEEN WHAT YOU SAY AND WHO YOU ARE."

(A quote taken from the book Integrity Selling: How to Succeed in Selling in the Competitive Years Ahead — by Ron Willingham, page 99.)

For years sales professionals had a reputation of saying what their prospects wanted to hear, and then resorting back to business as usual. Politicians have honed this skill to perfection.

The sad truth is that this poor reputation has been earned over the years. That is why most people, regardless of the industry, do not cozy up to the notion of "selling." Salespeople cannot be trusted. Salespeople have their own agenda. Salespeople talk too much and listen far too little. Salespeople disappear as soon as the sale is made.

You are a salesperson. How does this make you feel? I am a salesperson and I know how it makes me feel. Insulted.

Buyers are not stupid. They are very familiar with salespeople and how the poor ones operate by chasing their quotas and trying every trick in the book to:

1) Overcome objections
2) Upsell their products, and
3) Close every deal they can for the most profit.

<u>But you are not like this</u>. You are a good, honest, hardworking, caring person whose single goal is to help people make better buying decisions when it comes to travel. The fastest and most reliable way to position yourself as the good person you are is to "walk your talk." Be real. Show your prospects and clients a congruence between what you say and who you are.

To borrow from another book I once wrote ..... ***BECOME THE EXCEPTION***.

56. "Lazy" Is Not a Flattering Characteristic

I was speaking with a seasoned travel professional the other day when he mentioned something that caught my attention. He shared a recent event with me. He was having lunch with a group of agency owners who shared the same affiliation when a common thread emerged from the conversation.

He said all but one in the group mentioned that over the last ten months they have become lazy when it came to focusing on their businesses. They were having trouble getting back on track and performing the daily tasks that twelve months ago came naturally. They had lost or were losing their passion as each day unfolded.

For obvious reasons they now had time to concentrate on more personal activities and found enjoyment in performing non-work activities. This came as no surprise to me as the last twelve months have affected us all in deeply personal ways.

He went on to mention a concept that I am all too familiar with. He said that he felt it was high time to get back to basics. One word shot into my mind at this point. **BRILLIANT!**

The first step in achieving difficult tasks is to recognize the fact that perhaps you have been selling yourself short. Call it being lazy or call it lacking motivation. As you ponder the conundrum, you just might refer to it as a lapse in direction or a failure to see the big picture.

All that we have been experiencing over the past months and all we have been doing other than providing travel-related services paints a clear backdrop for the problem at hand.

Today I will simply say that becoming lazy is not something you invented. We all have been lazy to some degree. It has become another by-product of COVID-19. By simply recognizing this less-than-attractive behavior you (we) are well on our way to filing it as soon-to-be **"yesterday's news."**

Becoming lazy in times like these may be considered a common practice but it should in no way, shape or form be construed as a good thing. A sure-fire way to begin shaking yourself out of what appears to be lazy behavior is to begin accumulating "small" wins again. Start recognizing and enjoying the little things you are doing right.

In tomorrow night's story I will share a few of my own ideas on how to overcome the laziness factor.

57. Are You Becoming Lazy? Part Two

Last night I shared what I believed to be a common conundrum among travel professionals as COVID-19 continued to hinder people's travel plans. To be more specific, there seems to be a tendency for us all to become "tired" when it comes to performing the needed duties associated with building a business.

At the root of the problem is the fact that for the past twelve months we have found the time to enjoy the tasks that we consider to be more fun, more rewarding, and less frustrating or stressful.

Although we have succumbed to the problem, we now must "snap out of it" to borrow a phrase from the movie **MOONSTRUCK** staring Cher and Nicholas Cage.

In simple terms, becoming less lazy calls for being more active. So the question surfaces: How can we do what needs doing and actually enjoy the process? The answer is simple: By doing what works and what pays visible dividends.

The initial step is to begin envisioning your business as what it truly can be. You can rebound and become a profitable entity, if that is what you really want to happen. Then it becomes a matter of "small wins." Logically follow the path that will lead you to profitability. And this brings me to my ear-torn, sure-fire piece of advice that you can take to the bank. **"Become more visible."** Like it or not, you must come out of hiding and put yourself on the firing line. You must be seen. You must bring your assets to your marketplace. You must be heard. You must openly and freely share your knowledge with those who are interested.

I sometimes find that a simple change of pace and/or direction is enough to put a little bounce back in my step. A phone call to an upbeat friend or associate often is enough to reignite my "mojo." Perhaps a podcast is in your future. The options are all available .... and up to you.

But once you begin "experimenting" again and hitting on a few success stories, your energies will kick back into high gear and before you know it you will be doing your "happy dance" once again. (Remember, you must dance like nobody's watching.)

Lazy is for slugs, and you are not a slug. All you might require is a little nudging in the right direction to get you back in the game. Little wins. Step-by-step. Always moving toward your target. Tomorrow will soon be one of the "good ole days."

The good ole days are still in front of us.

58. The Good Ole Days Are Still Ahead

Tonight, I decided to call your attention to a valid sales lesson buried in a conversation I had last week with a travel professional.

This person was showing a sincere interest in joining our (Stuart Cohen and mine) Mastermind Retreat in Cancun this past March. I was reviewing the program when the agent mentioned the following.

"I am familiar with both of your and Stuart's work and feel very comfortable I will be receiving meaningful and timely information and stimulation. But the primary reason for my deciding to attend your Mastermind has much to do with the attractive "social aspect." Being a small (one-person) company, spending focused time with like-minded agents who are willing to openly share their information and experiences is downright exciting to me. "

BINGO! Feeling lonely and isolated takes its toll. You'd be hard pressed to find a better reason to attend an industry conference and to "get away" for a few uninterrupted days to recharge and adjust the future direction of your travel company with other like-minded professionals.

Think about it. In like fashion, it will soon be time for your clients and future prospects to realize that the best therapy for them after being holed up at home for so many months is to venture out and begin enjoying the beauty of our world again. And yes, many people have forgotten what a beautiful planet we live on. If a number of wars couldn't change that fact, neither will COVID-19.

I closed last night's story with the following sentence, and I will repeat myself today.

THE GOOD OLE DAYS ARE STILL IN FRONT OF US.

59. "Flying Around The Water Tower"

Picture yourself at 2500 feet above the ground sitting in a Volkswagen Bug with wings. You are at the controls of a Cessna 152 single engine airplane sitting next to an FAA inspector who has your future as a pilot in their hands. At the moment you have their life in your hands, but since this model airplane has two yokes that really is not the case.

Today was the day I had been training for, studying for, cramming for, practicing for and looking forward to. Today was the day. And I felt I was ready.

One of the tests is to take into consideration the four forces of flight: weight, lift, thrust and drag. The strength and direction of the wind also come into play. The test is to pick an object on the ground and maneuver your aircraft in a perfect circle around that object keeping it below the tip of your left wing. In my case, I picked a water tower in Haddonfield, New Jersey.

Three times around holding position was the objective. I flashed back to my studies. When you are flying into the wind, do this. When the wind is to your back, do that. When it is coming from the left, adjust with slight pressure. When from the right do the opposite.

I began my first turn. I was about to experience the wind from four different directions in a short period of time. The wind was slowing me down speeding me up, sliding me to the left and sliding me to the right. I kept circling but the tower was no longer below my wing. In fact it was a mile away by now. My mind was in a spin as I tried to figure out where I went wrong.

The instructor simply said, "Now go back and do it again." I did. Same results. She repeated herself, "Go back and do it again." Same results. My mind was spinning frantically. I was about to fail the test.

That is when she told me in no uncertain terms something I will never forget as long as I live. "Go back there and forget everything you ever read about making coordinated turns and fly this box around the &*%& water tower." And that is exactly what I did. Three times. Perfect. Tower holding steady right below my left wing.

Lesson: There is no substitute for studying, reading, practicing, researching and thinking. But when all the preparation is finished and done, it is time that you simply grab the bull by the horns and **"fly around the water tower."**

****Tonight's story ought to set you up for an interesting dream or two.

Bottom Line: Think. Study. Practice. Do.

60. Marketing Is Not For The Lazy

Why is building a profitable business so difficult? This is an easy question to answer.

And it has nothing to do with the Internet.

It is glaringly obvious to me that most people are still not practicing the simple art of marketing with any degree of consistency. Because there was (is) so much print on the subject, people are not being introduced to the finer (simpler) points of marketing in a fashion that is being taken seriously. There seems to be too much print on the "new flavor of the month."

My focused observations confirm that people either do not know enough to be concerned about marketing, or they think they already know all there is to know on the subject. That happens to be a popular error. We feel that since we have heard it before, we are good to go.

The truth is that knowing is not doing, and until we do, we don't know. "Knowing" might get you a gold star in the classroom. "Doing" pays the rent.

This lack of focused marketing activity introduces what I consider to be an enormous opportunity to educate the masses in the Marchev-Style of Edutainment. You can define this as business-building content with a giggle.

Copycat Marketing. One of the reasons marketing gets a bad rap is because many folks opt for the easy way out. And the easy way is to copy others who call whatever it is they are doing, marketing.

If you want a textbook example of what I am talking about, focus on your favorite airline – if there is such a thing. I'll never understand why each airline has a Marketing Director. Exactly 24 hours after one guy/gal makes a creative marketing decision, all 5000 competing airlines follow in step and do the exact same thing. Incredible! Prices up. Prices down. Wider seats. Narrower seats. Penalties for this. Penalties for that. Charge for bags. Sell the napkins. If one does it, they all do it.

If you simply copy what isn't working for others, you are going to be disappointed while finding yourself without working capital in very short order. You will also find the time to watch all 180 episodes of *Seinfeld* reruns. Twice! As entertaining as this may be, it is not a sound formula for a bright future in business.

My recommendation: ***Do not play "me-too." Do not sit and wait for your good fortune to materialize. Get up. Get out, and make your future happen.*** Start by telling more people that you are standing by to make their life easier.

61. "The Hay Is In The Barn"

It is a sad truth that some (many) people do not believe in paying their dues, doing their homework or paying the price that comes with success. Expecting something for nothing is a game for fool's, but many opt to take part in that game just the same. I was never a fan of rewarding our children with a trophy for just "showing up," or knowing how to put the baseball cap on with the bill facing forward. (I blame us baby-boom parents for this "instant gratification" thing we all have to deal with.

This subject came to light when I read an incoming email reminding me that there is plenty of opportunity out there waiting for the **prepared person**. It was Louis Pasteur who reminded us, **"Chance Favors The Prepared Mind."** The translation of these five words is "The harder you work, the luckier you'll get."

What does this have to with hay or barns you ask? Here is where I segue to tonight's lesson. It was back in 1968 when I first heard the term, **"The hay is in the barn."** Those six words were uttered each Friday afternoon the day before my UMASS football cronies and I took the gridiron to showcase our skills against some formidable opponent.

What our coach was telling us was the time to prepare was over. It was now time to play some football. And with this memory in mind my friends, it is now your turn.

I am assuming I am not speaking to a fingers-crossed want-to-be do thee well. I'd like to think I am speaking to a hard-working, honest, dues paying, fun and enthusiastic travel professional. I am talking to you, an exceptional human being.

It is time to ply your trade. Of course you will continue to be receptive to both learning and growing as an individual. But you already have all you need to get up, get out and start helping more people begin to enjoy the beautiful world we live in.

You have done your homework. You have completed the research. You have fortified your supplier relationships. You have considered all the options and alternatives. You have a Plan "B" in place, and you have waited your turn. Now the time has come for you to ply your trade. It is game time.

Your hay is in the barn. It is time to start playing the game you have come to love.

62. The "Deadliest" Sales Mistake

I know what you're thinking! How can I isolate the single most glaring error a professional can make in the field of salesmanship? You are probably wondering right now about the myriad of possibilities to choose from, including lack of follow-up, talking too much, inconsistency, failure to listen, and a hundred more sales-related miscues, as well as the more obvious business-killing turn-offs.

But there is one mistake that stands head and shoulders above the rest. In my 37-plus years of "carrying the bag," I have yet to uncover a sales mistake that even comes close to the "deadliest mistake." The irony is that this mistake, along with most of the others, can be avoided. In fact, they all can be prevented with just a little understanding coupled with some degree of intelligence.

Are you ready for this career-changing, life-altering, blinding flash of the obvious? Then here it is: **Stop being boring!** Decide once and for all to never again be misconstrued as a bore. Yes, it is time to pump a little positive personality into your game.

Let's dig a little deeper into this topic. What exactly is a bore? Any behavior that smacks of whining, negative complaining, people-bashing, crying, whimpering, or fault-finding can be construed as boring. In other words, avoid the normal everyday behavior of many, if not most, of the people walking around our country these days.

Most of us are tired of hearing about your personal war stories and would rather spend our time licking our own wounds and tending to our own personal baggage. Feeling sorry for "me" is a lot more appealing than being expected to feel sad about *your* problems. That's why I'm now going to introduce you to five preventive strategies designed to put you back on the high road to future success.

Know how the game is played.

I call it a game because at times in life it will appear that there is a winner and a loser. This is my way of reminding you that some days will be better than others. On some days you will be the windshield, while on others you will be positioned as the bug. Get it? You will have ups and downs. Go with the flow. Life exhibits the path of a sine wave.

Be an idea generator.

Your ideas may not all be million-dollar classics like the Pet Rock or the Hula Hoop, but one thing is for sure: Ideas, regardless of their shape, color or size, are never boring. I challenge you to walk up to anybody enthusiastically proclaiming you have a great idea. I bet you dollars to doughnuts that what you won't hear in return is this: "That's too bad. I'm sorry to hear that."

Be an idea supporter.

The sad truth is that most people feel it's their God-given responsibility to burst other people's balloons. Don't be one of these people. Instead, respond with a certain degree of interest to their idea with, "That sounds interesting. How are you planning to pull that baby off?" In other words, help them get excited about their brainchild by showing interest and support. Help them to expand on their initial brainchild.

Learn to laugh at yourself.

When push comes to shove, we're all pretty pathetic as we run hither and yon trying to figure out how life is supposed to work. Admit it. We all believe we're better looking than we are, smarter than we are, more creative, more understanding, more loving and better drivers. Get over it and start looking at yourself through a realistic lens. Chances are you are a mess just like the rest of us. Know it's okay to laugh at yourself.

Appreciate and applaud others.

This one is a "keeper," and worth the time you've invested in reading the first 61 bedtime stories so far. Follow this tip and you will position yourself as anything but a bore in your immediate world. Notice, appreciate, and applaud the good work and efforts of others. You will shoot to the head of the class in very short order.

We all watch the same news programs filled with the same bad news. We all struggle with the same daily problems and concerns. We are all grossly overworked and pathetically underpaid. We were all victimized by our parents' shortcomings and we feel persecuted in some way or another at some time or another. Some people are better at playing this game than others. As Cher tersely stated in the movie *Moonstruck*, **"Snap out of it!"**

But here's where the opportunity presents itself. If you can manage to distance yourself from the general rank and file and avoid boring, unappreciative behavior, you will position yourself as the one and only person to do business with. What have you got to lose? Become the exception. Stop being boring. Start acting like the winner you can be!

And you can introduce the new you to the world starting tomorrow. Good night.

63. Your Real "A" List

Turning suspects into prospects into customers is the way the sales cycle was designed. And in today's competitive sales arena, it takes a great deal of time and effort to see the cycle through to fruition. It takes time. It takes effort. It takes communication.

Once a prospect "raises their hand" and indicates an interest in what we are offering, I have always recommended you place this "HOT" prospect onto your **"A" List**. Then, it becomes your responsibility to cultivate your **"A" List** until the prospect becomes a customer or opts off of your list.

Your "A" List is made up of some very important people.
Prospects come and suspects go. Customers renew and you will lose some to attrition. The business beat will go on. But wait a minute .....just the other day, I was thinking about my **"A" List**. And then I started thinking about my **real "A" List**.

Who were the names on my **"A" List** that I would give it all up for? No company was on that list. Business is a great game, but it is not "*the*" game.

The names on my **real "A" List** consisted of names of "little" people. (Some not so little) The people who I am in position to really help and serve as a role model. The names on this list were Brian, Sara, Lauren, Megan, Will, Anne, Anthony, Michael, Mary, Cassidy, Andrew.

These are the names of my son, nieces and nephews. These are the people that mean a great deal to me. **These are the people on my real "A" List.**

Then I asked myself the same question I ask of business clients: If these people are so important to me, then when was the last time I sent a sincere and heartfelt communication to the people on my real **"A" List**?

This week's message comes as a question. When was the last time you communicated with your **real "A" List**?

And how often do you plan to communicate on a **REGULAR BASIS** moving forward? Not your business list. Your personal list -- the one that *really* counts.

Now for those of you who are not knee-jerking with a bunch of two-bit excuses about time, and blah, blah, blah, take a single name on you **real "A" List** and drop this loved one a "cold call" ... tomorrow. They will enjoy hearing from you, and you will have accomplished a great deal.

(Afterwards, you might want to drop a note to a valued client or two.)

64. People Are Watching. ("Walk Your Talk")

To set the table for tonight's message I would like to ask you a few questions. Answer these honestly without attempting to cover up your humanness. What are your initial thoughts when you come across these situations?

1. You see a stranger walk into a restaurant with a baseball cap on. He does not remove it as he takes his seat at the table.
2. You see a man walk to the passenger side of his car to open the door for his companion.
3. A stranger a good 20 feet in front of you holds the door open for you.
4. You spot a woman in a food store parking lot fails to return the empty shopping cart back to where she initially picked it up?
5. You see someone walking down a walkway stop to pick up some litter that was not their own.

No judgment on my part one way or the other. Each situation does merit a knee-jerk response, regardless if these are church-going people or not.

For years I have reminded you that people are watching you at all times and making decisions about your behavior. (Their decision. Their opinion.) These are just a few examples of daily activities that come to mind for the sake of example.

In addition to "everybody" espousing they provide exemplary customer service (which is a bunch of hooey) virtually everybody honestly feels that they "walk their talk." Which is also a bunch of malarkey.

In the past twelve months if you have not recognized the need for genuine, sincere and honest leadership then I have little more to offer in this or any future book. It is time for more people (you and me included ... us) to walk our talk.

Doing the right thing should not be as hard as many people make it out to be. The danger as I see it is when you decide to take the easy way because that is what everybody else is doing. And here is my take on this sad situation.

I believe that those of you reading this line of print are the "real deals." You don't take short cuts. You read. You listen. You study. You fail like the rest of us but you learn from each good-intentioned failure. The majority of travel "professionals" do not take the time or make the effort to improve themselves. They are not now reading my words, so there is no danger of my insulting them.

Bottom Line: People are watching you and making judgement calls. Walk your talk every day, as long as what you are saying is worth repeating.

65. Small Wins Lead To Big Results

Three days ago my sister sent me a motivational YouTube link from a Navy Seal outlining the ten most important steps to success. The initial step focused on "small wins." Twice in the same week from different sources one of my main topics of discussion were supported from without.

In the Seal speech, the drill sergeant shared the importance of beginning each day by making one's bed meticulously. The rationale was that if you started each day completing a task perfectly, it would set the tone for the rest of the day. It also reinforced the importance of executing with detailed precision.

Then came an audio book, which also supported the concept and value of the small win. Doing little things sooner than big things later was the major point of the chapter. It conjured up thoughts of a Casey Stengel quote I have been sharing for nearly 35 years. (NY Yankee & NY Mets Manager.)

"If my pitcher would pitch at the beginning of a game the same way he pitches at the end of the game once he realizes he is losing, he wouldn't be losing in the first place."

What can you do right now that will help your cause later? Something. Anything. In my case while I am training for a 70.3 Ironman Triathlon those "somethings" might include: A quick set of ten push-ups; a glass of water; twenty deep knee bends; 30 seconds of toe raises; a walk down and back up the steps to my condo.

In and of themselves, none of these carry a lot of weight. But not one of these maneuvers will hurt me. And in five months when it is "show time" I will be glad I took the time to continue my forward movement.

Small wins, incremental improvement, personal satisfaction in having completed a task properly is a mindset worth developing. Delete meaningless tasks and replace them with forward movement. Little-by-little. Onward and upward.

66. It Is Better Together

The other day I was listening to an interview with the popular marketing author Seth Godin. This gentleman has written over 20 books and has a style that comes across as genuine and easy to identify with. In short, I like this guy and I endorse the vast majority of his work.

A segment of the interview referenced how small businesspeople and entrepreneurs often slide out of sight while waiting for the magic pill to arrive next week, next month, or next year. He reminded the listeners that life in general is enjoyed more when sharing it with others.

Being a solopreneur myself, this short phrase caught my attention. I soon found myself agreeing that "two heads are indeed better than one" and that misery and success both enjoy company.

(I thought about how my small group of 65 travel agent professionals in my Inner Circle Sales & Marketing group meet every two weeks to share, listen, learn, and comfort each other.)

Seth then went on to support the concept of togetherness by saying like-minded individuals "enroll in the journey together." He went on to mention that the situation we all find ourselves in these days is in fact nothing more than a journey. The song made famous by Miley Cyrus popped into my head titled "**The Climb**."

The last phrase that Seth shared reminded me of the importance of candid and honest "sharing" when participating in a group.

Recapping the interview, (1) coming together, (2) enjoying the journey while (3) sharing experiences is the formula for everybody getting through the next twelve months and beyond.

Note: There is no benefit to me but based on my previous experiences with Seth Godin you might want to pick up a copy of his latest book titled **The Practice**. I just purchased the audio version and I'm looking forward to Seth's latest thoughts.

67. Take Time To Count Your Blessings

(Tonight's message was originally written around Thanksgiving time. It shares a valid reminder regardless of the month. I believe it is worth sharing with you tonight.)

Tonight's message may require a little explanation. But first I will share the catalyst that prompted my thoughts.

My wife received an email the other day with birthday wishes from a doctor she once visited. That in and of itself might have been considered a nice gesture. The last time she saw this doctor, however, was when she lived in New Jersey... and that was over twelve years ago. Isn't it amusing how computers can recollect important dates once an assistant finally gets back in front of an outdated database and hits the merge button with a pertinent "reminder?" *How heart-warming and thoughtful! (Not!)*

(Obviously, the cockles of her heart were not warmed that day.)

I have somewhat frowned upon Hallmark Cards serving as an over-priced influencer of thoughtful behavior. In my book, waiting for a holiday to tell somebody they mean something to you is nothing more than jumping onboard the "me-too" bandwagon. There, I have said it.

At the risk of appearing hypocritical, here I come. Today is the fourth Thursday of the month of November and is often referred to as THANKSGIVING. To some that means eating big. To others it may mean football. To a few others, nothing more than another day off from work. To me it is just one of 365 days that I wake up and count my many blessings.

I also take a moment to reflect on all those good, honest, hard-working people who might be spending the day feeling they have very little to be thankful for. I can't say or do anything to change their lot in life other than try to empathize with their situation. Some people are luckier than others and more fortunate through no fault of their own.

I was lucky the day I was born and I have been the recipient of luck ever since. Sure, Louis Pasteur went on record to remind us that "Luck Favors The Prepared Mind," and I suppose there is more than a modicum of truth in that statement. But regardless of the reason or fairness of it, I have much to be grateful for and I try earnestly to take nothing for granted. Who said, "There but for the grace of God go I."

As for the virus, it appears that help is on the way. The last twelve months have tested us in ways we never imagined. But if you are reading this very line tonight, it is proof positive that you have not given up yet.

If nothing else, you can be thankful that you are alive to fight another day.

68. You Can Start Tomorrow?

In a few short months we will be saying goodbye to another year and we will be getting ready to make the new year one we can be proud of.

Many of you reading this article today will be coasting through the rest of the year and drafting a list of good intentions for the next time around.

This is always the way it has been done, and it will stay that way for many years to come. But you and I are not like the others. We are one of the few. And as a result, we choose to do things differently.

The way I look at it, starting tomorrow, if we play our cards right, we can definitely distance ourselves from the competition.

Although I have a number of ideas for you to catapult yourself to the top of the hill, I realize that your resources and time constraints may prove my ideas to be empty suggestions at best.

What you do, how you do it, and to whom you do it to, is something you are going to have to come to terms with. There are many ways to skin a cat, and your future is just that ... your future.

So, tonight's story does not have a message per se. It comes in the form of a challenge for you to use the next 31 days to your best advantage. Please take time to think about where you want to be one year from today. Do yourself a favor and document your thoughts on paper. You don't have to share them with anybody, but by writing them out you will help clarify the work you have to do.

You may think that my stories are written for you. Nothing could be further from the truth. I will read and reread each chapter in hope that I will also benefit from the messages within.

Today was yesterday's tomorrow. Tomorrow will soon be here. Better than before.

69. Is Your Quality Controlled?

Not unlike many of my stories I want to feature a mistake I made recently in hopes that it will help you avoid similar future embarrassment, or worse. This one involved my daily column I once had with Travel Research Online.

It was on a Sunday night when I first realized I did not have an article for Monday morning's edition. I sprang to my laptop and begin documenting my thoughts as they entered my mind. All in all, I thought it was a pretty good last-minute piece. I hit the send button and for the next 12 hours I thought my life was back under control.

On Monday morning (the following day) I read the published piece and spotted more than a few typos. I immediately made the corrections and resent it by 10 AM. I tried to salvage my non-professional behavior as best I could. It did not have to happen. If I had only taken the time to give my article a final once-over, I would've spotted the errors before they hit the Internet.

In the overall order of disasters, I'm confident that my faux pas does not rate a spot in the Top 10. But my message to you remains the same. Start earlier, finish sooner. Give yourself time to review your work. There are 1 million reasons why holding focus has become more difficult than ever.

As a professional speaker this behavior particularly holds true. We always arrive at the meeting a day early to provide enough time to visit and review the meeting room set up from a-z. With enough time you can usually prevent any last-minute surprises.

That being understood, when you're dealing with somebody's vacation and are somewhat responsible for the money they are about to spend you cannot afford not to double and triple check your work.

On that particular Sunday evening I was not on my game. I hope it will serve as a l,esson for me to become a better writer in the months and years ahead.

70. A Lesson Worth Repeating

If you are an honest, hard-working business professional who has more than a modicum of interest in helping others get through this whacked-out world we live in, then I say it is your obligation to let us know you exist ... and are here to help us.

The secret is, (and keep this to yourself as it seems very few people know this) *you have to do something.*

- Piggyback your story off a well-publicized current event.
- Call local media personnel and ask them, "How can I help you?"
- Always keep your audience in the spotlight.
- Build your media mailing list TODAY.
- Simplify your systems.
- Know that publicity is not advertising.
- Find more fun ways to grow your business.

Every business professional knows the value of visibility, consistency, and being positioned as the go-to resource. I would be preaching to the choir if I began waxing eloquent on any one of these most important business truths.

But then again, if these truths are so self-evident, why do so many business professionals fail to get the message? Why does it take an uncanny number of whacks on the head for so many smart people to finally "get it?"

The simple fact is that, during a great portion of our adult lives, we all assume the role of "AIS." This is a softer, easier-to-accept term for the highly educated physician's name for the ever popular and quickly spreading Adult Idiot's Syndrome.

I want you to understand the following: PUBLICITY is free and it is a good thing for your business. Go get some.

But publicity is not about you or your business. It is all about the reader, listener, viewer, or recipient of your release. If you finally find the time to do your business some good at the expense of pushing a pile of papers from point "A" to position "B," then I want you to tell the recipient something (anything) they might want to hear.

Like how your company has recently announced the timesaving, vacation-saving, marriage-saving Special Report titled **How To Pack For a 2 Week Vacation Without Breaking Your Back or The Bank.** (There is not a married man over 30 who will not pay a week's salary to read these nuggets you jammed into this little jewel.)

Once you introduce new and exciting information, your audience can easily identify with and find to be of genuine interest, you are onto bigger and better things in the business world. You are now becoming the go to resource.

The media experts will be glad to include you in their programs because you are helping them. And according to me, that is exactly how the process is supposed to work.

Think of a whole bunch of stuff your audience wants (needs) to know. Remember that "wants to know" is more powerful than "needs to know." And while you are thinking, I want you to begin building your personal media database. This is nothing more than a list of local media contacts along with their address, phone number, email and if you are really getting into this thing ...***their golfing handicap***. (Just kidding.)

Then begin writing from the heart ... but shoot from the hip. Use little words. (But always, always, always be ready to dodge a handful of darts from some professorial guru-types who do not take misused hanging participles or gerunds requiring possessives very lightly.)

***For now, go to sleep. You can look up the word "gerund" tomorrow after your first cup of coffee.

71. Tell Me The Truth!

I don't know where I missed the boat. For the first 71 plus years of my life I always thought that telling the truth was the proper thing to do. For the past twenty years people from all walks of life, religions, political persuasions, industries, gender or shade of skin seem to have adopted the practice of telling lies... little white ones or otherwise.

I take exception to the oft uttered phrase, "As long as we are telling the truth, I ..." or "To tell you the truth, I ..." I would like to think that people are telling me the truth and that I don't have to question everything they say to me. The truth being ... I can't.

I drifted off topic today as I wanted to share my latest thoughts on "communication." It seems keeping people apprised of the current status of a project has become an outdated practice. "Multi-tasking" and being "too-busy" have become acceptable excuses for some. But not for me, and I hope not for you.

If you are going to do something, do it. If you don't feel you can get it done as promised, either tell me or don't tell me you are going to do it in the first place. I may not like the truth, but I have to deal with it. Stringing people on or taking advantage of their "understanding" is going to hurt you in the long run.

You might have guessed by now today's message comes from a recent episode I had with my builder. "I'll be there Tuesday." Tuesday came. Tuesday went. No call. No update. No apology.

After 71 years of laughing and scratching my way through life I have come to understand that "stuff happens." Tell me the truth. "You're running behind schedule. Your truck broke down. Your wife got mad at you and hid your keys." My staying home all day looking out the window waiting for a bathroom door to be delivered and hung as promised is not my idea of time well spent. **Talk to me.**

Let's turn the clock back a few years and surprise the bejabbers out of those in our circle. Let's be one of those who *always* tells the truth.

72. We Are Just Human!

I was reminded this week of a human frailty that I am guessing you and I have in common. At face value it is not bad although now that I focus on it, it is not very good either.

Let me try to set the stage by asking you a few questions.
(1) Have you ever registered for a webinar and failed to attend?
(2) Have you ever bought or requested a free E-Book or Special Report and never found the time to read it?
(3) Have you ever decided that you were going to contact, call or reconnect with a person of interest only to allow time pass without taking any action?

My guess is that you answered, "YES" to all three questions. So have I. I suppose we could spend the next few hours chastising our behavior in unison but that really wouldn't do either of us much good. After all, "**we are just human**." But, and I say "BUT" with all due respect, wouldn't it make more sense if we answered, "NO" to

all three questions. This brings me to a very important reminder. It involves the word "no."

With all the demands placed on your time these days there is one remedy that is easier said than done. Learning to say "no" to attractive opportunities may be the answer to your problem. Providing positive lip-service to anything or anyone and then failing to follow through can potentially tarnish your reputation.

From tomorrow forward, let us commit to only those tasks that we fully intend to complete. If you register for a webinar, show up ready to take notes. If you request an E-book or Report, schedule time to read it. When you want to connect with a friend, prospect, relative or client ... connect.

We just may be human, but we all can be better humans by saying what we do and doing what we say.

"Lights Out!

73. "Fine" Is Never Good Enough

When asked for a "four-letter word" that begins with the letter "f" most responses would rhyme with luck, duck and Chuck. I personally think this is one of the nastiest words used today and it seems it is being uttered by more and more people daily. There certainly are better words you could use. But if it were up to me, the four-letter word I am thinking of should be banned from the dictionary once and for all.

The four-letter word I am talking about that begins with the letter "f" is …. **FINE.**

"How are you feeling?" Fine.
"How was your salad?" Fine.
"How was your vacation?" Fine.
"How are your kids doing?" Fine.
"How was the service you received from your travel agent?" Fine.

Yuk! You can do a lot better than this. Fine in all the examples above implies, just okay, so-so, not bad, no complaints, it will do.

Right, wrong, good or bad, I have come to detest this word. I certainly do not want you to lie, but I just can't live with the reply "fine."

If you are in control of the event, you are in control of the response.
"Great, fantastic, incredible, super, second-to-none, simply wow, as good as it gets."

Here is the secret that too many people have failed to come to grips with.

If you want to hear great, give great. If you want to hear fantastic, give fantastic. If you want to hear incredible, give incredible. If you want to hear super, give super. (Are you getting the picture yet?)

The bad news is, and I am not apologizing for this, that from now on you will hear the word "fine" as it exits your mouth, and when you hear it said by others.

Although it may not be an official definition, one could say "fine" means "mediocre."
And I think you will agree with me, you do not want to be known as mediocre. I know I don't.

So, we have come to an understanding tonight. Starting tomorrow, "Fine" **is not** good enough.

74. Lessons From A Former Quarterback

Most people know what a football looks like. Many others actually know how the game is played and how the scoring works. Kicks, passes, blocks, runs and punts. Most people "get it."

But as good as you may be at watching a football game, what is "really" going on between the lines on both Saturday and Sunday afternoons may have you scratching your head in wonderment faster than a "quick slant on a silent count."

Having a little experience at the college level, I know a little bit about tonight's message. In fact, the University of Massachusetts thought enough of my quarterbacking skills to agree to pay for my education. (*The older I get, the better I was!*)

The game of football my friends is analogous to a game of chess. Eleven offensive pieces (positions) move in unison with the objective to cross a line at the end of the field where points are earned. This is commonly referred to as the goal line. The defensive players (pieces) do everything in their power to prevent this from happening.

The quarterback directs his "pieces" and decides how each one will contribute to the objective. He is the "driver" of the bus so to speak.

Here comes tonight's lesson. The quarterback spends 95% of his time scrutinizing the defensive unit. This is referred to as reading the defensive. He looks. He interprets. He decides. He calls the play. He watches. He adjusts. He repeats.

Here in lies the rub. If the QB spent his time focusing on his mechanics of (1) receiving the ball from center, (2) moving his feet in the right sequence and timing, (3) faking to the halfback, (4) assuming his position in the pocket (5) selecting a player to toss the ball to and (6) delivering a perfect chest-high spiral to his wide receiver, he would have been picking the grass from his face mask five seconds ago.

The QB's mechanics must be cemented in his every move requiring no additional thought on his part. His job is to clearly interpret what is going on on the other side of the ball so he can accurately "read" the safety and linebacker coverage before deciding in which direction to deliver the ball.

And so it is with you. **You are the quarterback of your business**. You are responsible for your forward progress until your business crosses the goal line. You must have your mechanics down pat in order to read your audience before deciding what avenue to take to better enhance your relationship with your clients and prospects.

Bottom Line: You must fine-tune your mechanics before listening, watching, and responding to the wants and needs of your audience. Study the opposition. Interpret their needs. Deliver the goods. Do your "happy dance." To coin a phrase from another sport, **"the ball is in your court."**

75. Your "Tone" Speaks Volumes

"THE LOOK IN YOUR EYE, THE SOUND OF YOUR VOICE, AND THE ENERGY THAT COMES OFF OF YOU AFFECTS EVERYBODY."

I came across this quote while reviewing a few of my past articles on a Saturday morning while I sat enjoying my morning cup of coffee. A recent experience came to mind and I believe it carries a message worth repeating. *Let me set the stage*.

I am beginning to train for a 70.3 Ironman Triathlon which is scheduled to take place in the northern panhandle of Florida in May. I covered the full 140.6 mile distance back in 1997 so this shortened version should be "a piece of cake." (But that was over 23 years ago.) At age 72 this just might prove to be a formidable challenge.

A significant training snag is preventing me from preparing properly for the bike portion of the race. My bike is in upstate New York and I am writing this article in southern Florida. In the world of tri-athletics this is referred to as a "conundrum."

My original plan consisted of having my sister and brother-in-law load the bike in the back of their car and drive down when they came south in early November. This plan fell through. It was time for Plan "B."

I blindly Googled bike shops near Utica, NY and made a phone call to an outfit called Trek Bikes. **Key point**: Trek sold bikes. I was not in the market for buying a bike." Here is where tonight's story unfolds.

I called to ask if I dropped my bike off at his bike shop, could he safely prepare it for shipping to an address in Florida. Knowing he was not a UPS Store franchise, and knowing I was not even going to buy a spare tire, I did not know what to expect from my inquiry. "**ABSOLUTELY**," was the next word I heard. Followed by "**EASY. BRING IT IN.** I remember hearing a sigh of relief on my end.

The "voice" on the other end of the line was upbeat, energetic, welcoming and both calming and reassuring. This was just a "voice" lacking any visible body movements to interpret one way or the other. No physical signs to sway my evaluation. No eye contact. There were no referrals to calm my uneasiness. Just a voice**. (The Power of The Voice.)** My initial impression was a favorable one to say the least.

The tone, clarity, interest, responsiveness, pauses and questioning skills were apparent and very much noticed and appreciated. This man's voice immediately put my mind at ease, and I knew I had found a solution to my dilemma. (Communicating properly, whether in person, online or over the phone should not be as difficult as many people make it.) When you experience it, you recognize it.

In a world where profits, multitasking, haste and self-gratification seem to have taken center stage, it is refreshing to find an organization that still knows how a winning hand is played. In most cases it all starts with your voice. (Doing it right does not require an advanced degree or equivalent.)

There is more to the story. If the service is rendered as promised, I will "gladly" pay the bill (labor and shipping) with no hesitation. And all I had to go on was a "voice" over the phone ... coupled to a delivered promise.

One other thing worth mentioning was the topic of insurance. In agreeing to box up and ship my bike, he mentioned he would be **insuring** the shipment at my expense without asking if I wanted to do so. He mentioned this in a "matter-of-fact" fashion as if this was not even a consideration. It was simply the smart thing to do. (Travel professionals, are you listening?) If I had other thoughts, I could have easily eliminated this fee. I did not. It was the smart thing to do.

My bike has not arrived yet in good working order so the final score has yet to be tallied. I have come to learn how to judge people pretty well over the past 40 years. My bet is on the voice (known as Jason) comes through with flying colors.

NOTE: Being in the sales profession for nearly 40 years I have come to realize that many salespeople have learned to "talk a good game" from the opening handshake. Once the sale is made, they dump you like a bad penny while moving on to the their next "target." I will be very surprised if I find Jason landing in that category.

Since writing this story, I am pleased to say that the voice known as Jason came through with flying colors. (I told you I could pick em.)

Don't ever underestimate the power of your voice. Your "tone" can speak volumes.

76. A Note To Myself

I met my stepson when he was seven. Brian is 45 today. Time certainly does fly, and as hard as that is to come to grips with, I consider it thoght to be a HUGE wake-up call. It is true: **"Time waits for no man."**

You are probably wondering what does this have to do with you, and why am I sharing this useless statistic with you. Maybe nothing. Maybe tonight's message is for me.

As many of my loyal readers have come to understand, I am a big fan of "repetition." At the risk of repeating myself for the umpteenth time, here comes a reminder that is worth remembering. I am sure you have heard it before.

Today's message is being taken from a sign I have hanging over my desk. It simply reads: **"WORK HARD TODAY TO AVOID DISAPPOINTMENT TOMORROW."**

And speaking of repetition, here is a quote I know you have heard from me before:

"If my pitcher would pitch at the beginning of the game, the same way he pitches at the end of the game ... once he realizes he is losing, he would not be losing in the first place."

This last quote came from Casey Stengel of baseball fame.

Both of these quotes serve as reminders that your actions **TODAY** will determine your progress **TOMORROW**. And while your bogus excuses and ongoing tendency to procrastinate may tempt you from time to time, your future is arriving far too quickly to waste any time. **To ensure better "tomorrow," don't screw up "yesterdays."**

Buckling down is certainly not the easy route to take. But in the long run, (which will prove to be the short run as time continues to fly), your life will be far better off by doing today what you want to put off until tomorrow. But, today is gone. So tomorrow is the day to put your plan into motion.

Author's Note To Self: I hate it when I read my own stuff and realize I am talking to me. It is 49 degrees outside and to avoid being called a hypocrite, I have to put on my swimsuit and head for the pool to swim for an hour.

May 15th will be here before I know it and if I want to finish the 70.3 mile Ironman Triathlon in a semblance of good order, I will have to **work hard today to avoid disappointment on race day**.

77. FCS: These Three Letters Will Help Run Your Business

During my daily walk I often listen to an audible book I downloaded over the past few months. The most recent title is a book called **Essentialism** by author Greg McKeown. In a nutshell this book reminds us to eliminate all but what is essential in our daily lives.

I'm not sure in what chapter I picked up the following three-letter reminder, but it struck a chord with me and I thought I would share it with you tonight.

The letter F stands for Focus. The author immediately brought up the topic of multitasking and contrary to what I have been sharing with you over the years, he thought multitasking was indeed possible. My definition of multitasking was **"How to screw up many things at once."** Mr. McKeown reminded me that you could indeed do two things at once. For example, you can do the dishes while listening to the radio. You can sing a country song while mowing the lawn. But what you cannot do is *focus* on more than one thing at the same time. And therein lies the rub.

Only by focusing on a single task can you do your best work. This brings to mind an old Chinese proverb that reminds us, **"Man who chases two rabbits catches none."**

The second letter C stands for Communication. With so much noise and information bombarding us each and every day, from all corners and segments of the media spectrum, it is no wonder that we learn to tune-out and take shortcuts when it comes to delivering and receiving important information. My suggestion is to follow Simon and Garfunkel's sage advice when they reminded us to "Slow down. You're moving too fast. You've got to make the morning last." (59th Street Bridge Song)

Don't just hear what I am saying. Take the time and make the effort to listen so you will understand what I am saying, and what I am not saying.

Letter S stands for Speed. And it is here where I remind you "he who hesitates is lost." People are used to having things delivered **now** rather than **later** thanks to companies like FedEx and Amazon. "Strike while the iron is hot" is my best suggestion to you if you are sincerely interested in growing a profitable travel business. Ideas come and ideas go in a New York minute. "When the student is ready, the teacher appears." (I think you are getting the picture.)

I must balance this "speed" thing with a counter point of view that reminds us that "haste makes waste." Balancing the two, speed and deliberation, appears to be the key to your success. They are easy to say, but harder to adopt as your ongoing personal strategy.

78. Pick Up The Phone. Make The Call.

Something happened recently during my Inner Circle Sales and Marketing Meeting that I wanted to share with you tonight. It was simple yet profound. It just may be an example of the most underutilized marketing tactic used today.

I was sharing my experience of placing a cold call to a highly recognized and respected person I wanted to meet after years of just "thinking about it." One day I picked up the phone and made the call. I asked for a lunch date and was genuinely surprised when the person agreed to meet with me.

After sharing the sequence of events at my meeting a number of travel agents chimed in and began to mention how much they enjoy listening to this very same person on her weekly podcast. I recognized this as an opportunity, so I contacted the woman to share the positive kudos she was receiving from my group.

Immediately following the meeting, I sent an email asking her to call me since I wanted to share something I thought she would like to hear. (The hook) Within 20 minutes my phone rang and we were sharing war stories while laughing freely.

She was genuinely flattered when I shared all the positive comments I had received earlier in the day. I then had an idea. I asked her if she could find a few minutes to email a few of my participants to personally acknowledge their thoughtful remarks.

Here is where tonight's lesson kicks in. She immediately said, "Why don't I give them a call on the phone instead of just emailing them?" WOW! I thought this was an incredible gesture ranking high above and beyond my expectations.

So as not to abuse the offer, I sent her just a handful of names and she indeed made each and every call. Each of the recipients were surprised and amazed she had taken the time to call them personally.

Each one of you reading this article today has both the opportunity and the capability to brighten your client's day with a quick phone call. Like most people, you probably feel that this simple gesture does not have any significant meaning. You are wrong.

Take the time and make the time to call your good clients and/or prospects to thank them for giving you the opportunity to work with them. Just a few calls a week will work wonders for your reputation.

I can only hope you will swallow your fears and give this idea shot. I am confident you will thank me for it. **Do Not Minimize The Power of The Phone Call.**

79. Pretty Close To a Proven Success Formula

In cleaning out an office draw last week I came across an old business card of mine. It brought me back to the days when my slogan was **TGIT: Thank Goodness It's Today.**

On the back of this card were 19 reminders split into three categories. Starting tonight, and for the next two nights, I will share my thoughts on each of these 19 reminders.

The first category was **SALES**.

1. **Pick a target**. You are spinning your wheels if you are still depending on sales being a numbers game. List the names(s) of your would-be next clients and then devise a plan to meet with them; talk with them; decide if you are in position to help them; help them.
2. **Ask more questions**—Then listen. You already know what you already know. You learn nothing new when all you hear is the sound of your own voice. Besides, most people like to hear the sound of their own voice so play their game. Get them talking. Then, and I am afraid this needs to be said, listen to what they are saying... and what they are not saying
3. **Be on time**. Then be brief. Salespeople are usually pretty good at being on time. It is a sign of respect and genuine interest. But salespeople are also pretty good at over-doing their stay. I will leave you with the sales professional's mantra: **BE BRIGHT; BE BRIEF; BE GONE**.
4. **Bring something of value to the party**. Don't always show up to "get" something. Show up with something to give and leave behind, with no strings attached. That something can be a meaningful bit of pertinent information or a small, inexpensive memento of some type. Bottom line: Just like house parties, you would not dream of showing up empty handed.
5. **Be the exception**. The world is filling up quickly with "me-too-only-better" people. They all look the same. They all sound the same. They all act the same. They all think the same... to a degree ... if they think at all.

   The golden opportunity is **NOW,** if you want to distance yourself from the competition. I can think of a hundred ways for you to do this, but I will leave you with just three to get you started.

   - Work on the sound and tone of your voice so it seems like you are actually happy to hear from me.
   - Do what you say you will do without hesitation or bogus excuses. (I know how busy you are, and I really don't care.)
   - When speaking with me, speak to me. I know how good you are at multitasking ... and I really don't care. When working with me, focus on me.

   Tomorrow night I will review eight **CUSTOMER SERVICE REMINDERS** followed by **MOTIVATION REMINDERS** on the next night.

80. Five Customer Service Reminders

Last night we touched on five sales reminders that will help put you miles ahead of your competition. Tonight, customer service will be our topic of choice.

The first three reminders are borrowed directly from The Ritz Carlton's famous reputation for superior customer service. Brace yourself for a blinding flash of the obvious.

1. **Say "hello" with enthusiasm**. People often judge you buy the first impression. And in most instances, the first impression has something to do with the sound of your voice. Therefore, doesn't it make sense to capitalize on this initial opportunity as best you can. By looking people in the eye and greeting them like you sincerely appreciate their presence will go a long way at initiating a meaningful relationship.
2. **"Anticipate" the future**. This is an area where you can shine immediately when compared to your competition. Thinking that they are better than they are, your competitors feel they can "wing" each situation as it arises. This truly is the self-destroying belief of an amateur.

    If you have been in the business for any period of time whatsoever you have noticed that there are only a few situations that surface repeatedly. By doing your homework beforehand and knowing how you will approach each problem as it presents itself, you will be silently showcasing your professionalism. I'm reminded of my often-repeated quote by Louis Pasteur when he reminded us that **"Chance Favors the Prepared Mind."**

3. **Say "good-bye" with sincerity**. Although first impressions may be important, last impressions create the lasting impression. Do not miss this opportunity to cement the relationship based on genuine interest and caring. Be sure to bid your guests a fond farewell and mean every word of it.
4. **Say "thank you" and mean it**. Contrary to popular belief you cannot say thank you often enough to the people who have made your business possible. Seek every opportunity to connect with your good clients, and make sure they know you have no intention of ever taking them for granted.
5. **Be a lifeguard**. Not unlike lifeguards down at the beach, or fireman waiting for the bell to sound, you want to be considered the "go-to" resource when things are not running smoothly. Over the years I have heard many travel agents complain when they are called upon in times of trouble. From tomorrow forward I want you to relish the fact that you are the one called when professionalism is at its utmost importance.
6. **Deliver... plus 1**. The term I use for this concept is "Lagniappe" which I believe is a French term which translates to *the cherry on top of the sundae*. In other words, after your job has been completed, what else can you do to "wow" your customer by surprising them with the unexpected. It is doing the "what's next," when the "next" is not expected. (We will finish the list tomorrow night with motivation. Until then ...)

81. Final Day of The Proven Success Formula: Motivation

As I warned you last night, what you are about to hear should not come as news. I am betting that you are not following through on these reminders. Please, prove me wrong. Tonight, we are going to discuss "motivation."

1. **Eat, rest, and exercise daily**. When push comes to shove and all other things are equal, you are *the* differentiating factor when selecting a service provider. Don't sell yourself short. You probably are taking better care of your pets and your motor vehicle than you are of yourself. Get enough rest, watch your calorie consumption and "move" your body to some degree every day.
2. **Set and achieve goals**. This is my way of reminding you of the importance of having a target to shoot at. Time passes too quickly, and David Cassidy's last words hit the nail right on the head when he said, ***"Too much time was wasted."*** Pick a goal. Work at achieving that goal. Pick another goal.
3. **Do your homework**. I think I said this the other night: **"CHANCE FAVORS THE PREPARED MIND."** Louis Pasteur said it, I endorse it. Regardless of how many years you have been in business, or how accomplished you are, winners continue to practice until it is time to "hang up their spikes." Another smart guy who escapes me at the moment said, "The harder I work, the luckier I get." Believe it.
4. **Celebrate achievements**. Take a lesson from our professional sports teams. They work hard all day with mostly nothing good happening. Then their skills pay off and they SCORE. And what happens? They jump on each other and beat the heck out their teammates in a quizzical form of celebration. But regardless of how you do it or what you call it, when you achieve one of your goals, find the time to acknowledge your success. **CELEBRATE.**
5. **Look for the fun**. I used to flash a slide at the beginning of my presentations of an older gentleman with the following quote referring to the meaning of life: "I am not sure why we are here," it read, "but I am pretty sure it is not to enjoy ourselves." **Balderdash.** Call me a reality contrarian but if it isn't fun, I'm not sure I "want in." I believe helping people is fun. I think taking an idea and seeing it through to a satisfactory ending is fun. I think making money is fun. I think it is okay to have fun. Let me leave you with two pieces of advice:

   (1) You can't win them all.

   (2) It is up to you to make your future both fun and rewarding.

82. What Does Calking a Bathroom Seam Have To Do With You?

A recent home remodeling project is responsible for tonight's message. My example may not be pertinent to you at this exact moment, but I think you will connect with tonight's message on your own terms.

One wall in our guest bathroom was recently tiled. It butted up against a newly painted adjacent wall. The resulting joint (seam) was not as clean as my wife would have liked, so we resorted to man's greatest invention ... **Quarter-round molding**.
(Next to the wheel, molding of any type is man's greatest invention and by itself has saved countless marriages from ending prematurely.)

I made a special trip to Lowes to purchase two 8-foot sections, which was ample linear footage to complete the job. That was easy. I painted each section with the same paint used for the adjacent wall. That was easy. I used "liquid nails" to fasten the molding in place. Once again, easy. I revisited Lowes to purchase a tube of grey calking in order to fill in the seams which would complete the job. Easy. **And here comes the message.**

That is when procrastination raised its ugly head. For reasons still unclear to me, I delayed snipping the tube of calk, applying a small bead, and smoothing it into the seams with my wet fingertip. My mind began to play games with me. What if it did not look good? What if I made a mess and made things worse than it was now? What if?

I allowed procrastination to enter the project as one day turned into the next. The truth of the matter was that what I had to do to finish the job was easy to do. It would take less than ten minutes. (Probably closer to five.) Yet, I found myself delaying the task that would complete the job.

What easy tasks are you putting off that need your attention for no logical reason? What is preventing you from wiping the slate clean and focusing on your next challenge? Chances are the thing that is holding you back has little to do with rocket science. All you need to do is ... do it ... and it will be done with.

I have often reminded you that **"the mind quits first."** Calking a bathroom seam is easy, yet my mind was telling me otherwise. A root canal promised to be less taxing at the moment. This was nonsense.

Starting tomorrow do what you have been putting off. Send me an email applauding your self-discipline. mike@mikemarcev.com In return, the next time we talk, my calking job will be an event of the past, and my marriage will still be intact.

83. Mediocrity Is Not a Good Thing

I was thinking about this word the other day, (mediocrity) and for reasons unknown to me I connected it with the travel industry. Maybe it had something to do with a previous article I wrote focusing on doing things above and beyond that which is expected. I am sad to say that the "expected" involves more than simply showing up. On the other hand, the "unexpected" demands attention, determination and a certain degree of creativity.

To borrow from a book titled with the same reminder, the secret is to **Become The Exception**. Like all good advice and good intentions, this is easier said than done. Allow me to explain.

me·di·o·cre [mee-dee-oh-ker] adjective
1. Of only ordinary or moderate quality; neither good nor bad; barely adequate.

You certainly do not want to be considered as mediocre. Rather than starting to defend yourself, let it suffice to say that "if" this is true -- then service in America has become barely adequate. This implies that an enormous opportunity presents itself. If this shoe doesn't fit, how about taking the synonym approach? Undistinguished, commonplace, pedestrian, everyday; run-of-the-mill. I don't know about you, but I want none of these labels on my tombstone.

Let's look at the flipside ... the opportunity. Antonyms include extraordinary, superior, uncommon, incomparable. *Now you're talking*.

Thirty years ago, I seized an "opportunity" that was introduced to me and I penned an easy-to-read book on the importance of *becoming the exception*. It was fun to write and even more fun to read. The good news is that after 5000 copies have ,sold, and nearly thirty years later, my messages still hold water. The information today is as relevant as it was back then. Fundamentals don't go out of style. The basics still hold the key to your future success. Mediocrity will always remain a shortcut to ... nowhere.

84. The Power of The Well-Executed "Launch"

If you are looking for a good business book to read, I recommend Jeff Walker's **Launch**. It reminds us of the importance if timing and the value of "setting up" your next important project. I was introduced to a great example of how "anticipation" works earlier today.

Stuart Cohen and I are training for an Ironman 70.3 Triathlon along with a mutual friend of ours, Frank Adornato. The race was scheduled for May but they were postponing registration for some time. Since this was a rescheduled race, and we were not originally planning to compete, we were beginning to fear that the regularly allotted positions would be taken.

We heard through the grapevine that registration would open soon. This race had four tiers of registration; each one with a different price point. We wanted "in," but at a price we could afford.

I remember it like it was yesterday. We were told that registration would open at 12 noon. At 11:55 am we were positioned at our computers ready to pounce. 11:58... 11:59 and then twelve noon. We were on the website ready to handover our credit card numbers when nothing happened. 12:01.... nothing. 12:05 .... nothing. Then at 12:07 the registration link became "*live*."

As we frantically filled out the form with phone numbers, shirt sizes, age, emergency contact names and numbers and finally our credit card numbers, we began to sweat in hope that our computers would transfer this information to the race computer and automatically send our confirmation number. We waited. And waited. And then came the good news. We were instantly out a lot of money and were committed to making our lives extremely uncomfortable for the next four and half months.

If there was no downside to waiting until we got around to it, who knows what the final outcome would have been. If registration had been open for months, who knows if we would have procrastinated and decided one day to pass on this opportunity.

The fact that we had to wait before ensuring we had a spot on the starting line added to the suspense and excitement. As it turned out, we were wishing, hoping and praying that somebody would take our money and grant us entry. I don't know about you, but I find this to be slightly strange behavior. "Please take my money... please."

And so it is with you and your next group meeting, trip, cruise or adventure. Don't dump your wagon prematurely. Set it up with benefits. Promote the details ... and wait.

Get your potential participants chaffing at the bit to "pull the trigger." Advertise a date when your registration will open along with different tiers of pricing. Begin the countdown. Then "OPEN" for business. If you play your cards right, your gig will sell out in record time.

85. Kaizen Revisited

Kaizen is a Japanese word meaning "improvement." I like to think of kaizen meaning **"incremental improvement."**

I was reminded of this concept this morning. When I get up, my aging body reminds me that ... *my body is aging*. Every muscle, tendon, limb and synapse connected to my brain tells me to move slowly lest I injure myself on the way to the bathroom. How could things have gotten this bad? I blame it on age coupled to a lack of activity. I suppose a lack of discipline over the years could have something to do with it.

You may not know this about me. After thinking about it for the past twenty years, I have recently decided to make another attempt at competing in an Ironman competition. (A triathlon covering 70.3 miles consisting of three individual events; swimming, biking and running.)

Little by little I am introducing my body to the stresses of rigorous "movement." I must say this challenge is easier to select as a goal than to making it a reality. Every morning my body screams at me as I swing my legs off to the side of the bed.
UNTIL TODAY.

Today when I got up I actually felt like a human being. I said to myself quietly enough as to not wake my wife, ***"What's up with this?*** I actually feel good." As I nuked a cup of milk and prepared to add some Ovaltine it dawned on me. Kaizen was working for me.

Kaizen had silently entered my training picture and proved my understanding of the concept as being correct. After 60 days of gently getting back into some semblance of condition, the daily regimen of bending and stretching was finally paying off. Step-by-step, stretch-by-stretch, stroke-by-stroke my muscles were beginning to respond favorably as I had hoped they would. I must admit I expected faster progress. (Wishful thinking on my part.)

Lesson time: You too must put your faith in the kaizen approach regardless of your next challenge, project, assignment or mission. Whatever you choose to do next will most likely take longer than you first expected. In the beginning you will exhibit some form of discomfort as you ease into the project.

The key is to continue taking those small steps in the right direction. At first, you might feel you are fighting an uphill battle. Your mind will suggest daily that you your next best maneuver would be to "throw in the towel." When this happens, repeat the word "kaizen" to yourself. Stay the course. I promise you good things lie just ahead although they may currently be out of sight.

One day, as if my magic (like it happened to me this morning) you will begin to see the light at the end of the tunnel and you will soon experience the fruits of your labor paying off.

86. Don't Sell "Snail Mail" Short

Like everything in life, there are two sides to every coin. My observation will not sit well with everybody reading tonight's message, but it will pertain to many of you.

I was sitting at my desk the other day when I glanced out the window and spotted one of my older neighbors shuffling toward the mailbox. I watched hoping I would not have to run to his aid should he stub his toe and take a tumble.

He made it unscathed to the mailbox and inserted his key. Upon opening the box I saw him lean down and peer into an "empty" box. He closed the box and shuffled back to his apartment with no news, good or bad.

A second example comes from my own apartment. Everyday my wife asks me if I spotted the mailman drive by. For Barbara, a daily trip to the mailbox is an anticipated part of her day.

Why am I sharing this with you tonight?

The old fashion envelope may not "float the boat" of the younger set, but I am here to tell you that anybody over the age of 50 still enjoys risking a paper cut when opening up an envelope.

I know email is faster. I know text messages are cheaper. I know most of you have forgotten how to use a telephone. I also know that for a certain demo and psychographic, the stamped envelope still holds a valuable spot in your marketing mix.

And here is what I consider to be somewhat amusing. Maybe downright sad better explains it. A large percentage of my readers will find themselves agreeing with today's message. The majority of these good people, however, will not send a single letter in the next 30-days.

Some smart guy once said, "You can lead a horse to water, but you can't make it drink."

I am suggesting with solid data supporting my assertion, that people look forward to receiving mail and will read what you send them.

If you want more customers, try sending more snail mail.

87. It Is Time That You Make Your Move

Before calling it another day, I would like to share two experiences with you. They have nothing to do with each other, but both serve as good reminders.

The first one occurred during my biweekly Inner Circle Meeting. The meeting ran a full 70-minutes but by the reports I later received indicated we accomplished a great deal. It wasn't until I signed off at the end of the meeting that I realized that I had neglected to hit the record button. Since many of my members rely on the recording you might imagine how I felt as result of this oversight. The word I used was **DUMB**!

The first lesson involves checklists and quality control. These meetings have become second nature to me and although I consider myself a professional, I was reminded how the adult mind can easily overlook important details. I knew I was supposed to record the meeting. I forgot.

This is where you come in. You serve as your client's safety net. Your job is to make sure that their "record button" gets pushed; the small print is read on the contracts; and every detail from a A-Z is examined and approved, reviewed and addressed.

Lesson Number Two.

Later in the day I received an email from an agent who I have not had the pleasure to meet personally. She connected with one of my daily messages and took the time to reach out to me to show her appreciation and interpretation of this particular article. The key phrase here is *"took the time."*

Here was my opportunity to return the courtesy and let her know that people do read her emails. I dialed her phone number and left a "thank-you" message on her voice mail. Minutes later my phone rang and for the next fifteen minutes two "strangers" had a delightful conversation.

Ladies and gentlemen, opportunities to spread goodwill and showcase your professionalism are everywhere. You just need to remove your blinders, stop worrying about what "might" happen, start focusing on what "could" happen and *make your move*. This is simple stuff. If you want more all you have do is do more.

I will leave you with just five reminders:

1. Have your client's back. Be their "centerfielder." Be there for them.
2. Make your move sooner rather than later. (Speed)
3. Exercise more / Talk less
4. Don't ever lose your sense of humor
5. Be humble and kind.

88. "I Know You're Busy So I'll Let You Go!"

A phrase I find somewhat humorous (not) while talking on the telephone is one you might be familiar with. **"I know you're busy, so I'll let you go."** Translation: "I'm done talking to you. I have better ways to spend my time. Gotta go. Ta-ta."

I am reminded of a popular Yogi Berra saying that reminds us **"It's not over 'til it is over."** Remember, your conversations are not over until they are over. This is particularly apropos if you are interested in making a favorable "lasting impression" when speaking to both prospects and current clients.

I'll cut to the chase and leave you with tonight's reminder. **DON'T RUSH YOUR "GOOD-BYEs" ON THE TELEPHONE**. First impressions may be important, but it is the "last" impression that is the most memorable. Most people can tell when they are receiving "the bum's rush." You have worked too hard to screw up any good relationship simply because you choose not to close the conversation favorably.

Allow the person on the other end of the line to completely finish their last thought. Then in a slow and sincere tone thank the caller/callee for their time. Then pause before saying good-bye. And here comes the magic: **DO NOT HANG UP BEFORE THEY DO.**

89. Ready Or Not Here Comes Tomorrow.

Here are the facts. Today has come and gone. Mentally, politically and financially, it is done. Over. Caput.

The one and only question worth asking is "What are you planning to do with tomorrow? I've said it before, and I will say it again. You are driving the bus. Where you take it is entirely up to you.

One thing is for sure. There is not a shortage of people, websites, podcasts, documents and pdf's, both online and off, suggesting the many ways for you to grow your business. I think the popular term is TMI. (Too much information.)

I am taking this factoid to heart and have decided to "back off" as to the volume of information I will be sending your way in the coming few months. For five years I have been writing a daily column for Travel Research Online but will now offer a weekly kick-off article. My new column will be called **Mike's Monday Cup of Mo-Joe**.

Translation: A morning cup of motivational food-for-thought.
By definition "mojo" is defined as magic. And what better environment to help you kick

off the week than over a cup of coffee on Monday morning. Get it?

I reserve the right to discuss, report on, or refute any timely topic that I feel will help you feed your families. As they say down at the nets, "the ball is in my court."

In addition to my **Monday Cup of Mo-Joe**, I will continue to share timely information on my Thursday Podcast titled **Mike'd Up Marc**hev. All future and archived episodes can be found at www.TravMarketMedia.com

90. Would've - Could've - Should've

Don't allow yourself to fall victim to this behavior:

- I would've done it if I had more money.
- I could've tried if I had more time.
- I should've called them but ...

This happens more often than not when you get an idea and fail to act on it. Excuses seem to present themselves with your buying into them. This simply does not have to happen.

Once you have an idea for a notion to do something, do it. Don't think it to death. And don't procrastinate until you forget what it is you were going to try.

I have always said that one of the most powerful words in English language is the word "Idea." Ideas are good things. Ideas are exciting things. Ideas are intriguing things. Ideas are fun to have and fun to try. People like to hear about ideas. My advice to you is to conjure up more ideas and then act on them.

Not all ideas work. Most ideas won't work. As a matter of fact, most ideas don't even leave the new idea launching pad.

My advice remains the same. Work on generating more ideas. Then share them with your prospects and customers. In other words, I want you to propose a few action thoughts with people you wouldn't mind doing business with.

"Blow in their ear." Say something to them that might even lead them to having an idea or two of their own. (Heaven forbid!)

Be careful though. This will soon become an addictive habit. You will soon be having so much fun that you will be making this a way of life... *a regular thing*.

Once you begin acting on your ideas you will eliminate the words would've, could've and should've from your vocabulary.

Have a good night. (I have a better **IDEA**.) *Make it a GOOD NIGHT.*

91. The Four D's. (Four Words Leading To Your Success)

The swimming pool in my condominium has recently reopened and I slip into the water by 9 am every morning and with rare exceptions, I share the pool with just one other fellow. My swimming buddy is Frankie "Cheech" who spends the summer months in New Jersey. (Maybe that is why we understand each other so well while sharing a similar sense of humor.) I was raised near Exit 142.

The other day Frankie called my attention to four words he learned while in the service. (Rest easy. They are acceptable in social settings.) We have come to refer to these words as the "Four D's." I have positioned them as my guiding reminders. They keep me on track and help me stay focused while I train for an upcoming event. (I'm preparing my aging body for an Ironman 70.3 Triathlon.)

The Four D's Are: Desire; Determination; Dedication & Discipline. I have imbued these four words in my brain and recall them when I find myself seeking permission to take shortcuts with my training.

I think these four words may pertain to your personal quest as you strive to build and maintain a thriving travel business. Let's break them down.

Desire. The dictionary defines desire as "wanting, wishing, craving and yearning." This is where it begins, but by no means end. Knowing what it is you want to accomplish is key. It is an important first step. But "talk is cheap." We have to make our dreams happen. **You want a profitable company filled with appreciative clients**. Now what?

Determination. In another word ... willpower. To accomplish anything worthwhile we need to introduce commitment to the equation. Grit, purpose, fortitude and resolve are what serves as positive traits leading toward the fulfillment of our dream. Nothing can get in your way. **Nothing will stop you from serving your niche.**

Dedication. I am not suggesting that you become a "one trick pony." I am saying that "focus" and "single-minded" dedication will be what gets you to where you want to go. With the proper mindset, the challenges you will be facing will be nothing more than small speed bumps. They may slow you down a bit, but you will never have to stop. **Keeping your eye on the target while deploying tunnel-vision will prove to be your strong suit.**

Discipline. This is the glue that holds your dream together. You have heard me say repeatedly **"the mind quits first."** There will be times when you will want to quit. You will find yourself questioning your chosen path. You will speak negatively to yourself, and worse yet, you will start listening to these negative thoughts. Even worse, you may even start believing what you are hearing. Don't do it. You mustn't do it. You can't allow your own negative self-talk to sabotage your future accomplishments.

Whether you like it or not, whether you feel like it or not, whether your efforts are lacking any sign of accomplishment, you must remember that you are "driving the bus." You are at the controls of your destiny. And as mystical as it may sound, your body will always follow your head. **You do things you do because it is time to do them**.

You might want to do what I did to make sure the **Four D's** are not forgotten. Print them out on a small card and keep it in your wallet. Tape it on your bathroom mirror. Position it on your car's dashboard.

NOTE: More logical business-building reminders can be found at **Mike'd Up Marchev**. My weekly podcast is archived at www.TravMarketMedia.com.

92. Get Yourself In Position To Win

An accident on the last lap of the Daytona 500 resulted in victory for driver Michael McDowell who had no chance to win until then. After 498 miles of racing this driver found himself "in position" to take advantage of a last lap pile up. The result was a trophy and a large sum of money.

The lesson was glaringly clear. If you ever want to have a chance to win as a result of the unexpected, you had better find a way to get yourself in "position." Opportunities often evaporate as fast as they appear. You must be able to respond in a flash before giving your opponent room to rebound.

Michael McDowell did not have the fastest car. He was not the most talented driver. For 499.5 miles he never was in the lead. But at the end of the race, he was the winner. Why? He was in position to take advantage of the unexpected.

I remember a similar occurrence years ago in the Winter Olympics. The event was Short Track Speed Skating. Apollo Ono was a household name at the time. After jockeying for position through the final race there was a last lap slip as the lead skaters smashed into the side-board. The "last" place skater was unaffected, and he stayed on his feet and finished the race ... in first place. This Canadian-born long-shot went home with the Gold. I interpreted this as another example of being in position when the opportunity presents itself.

My final example supporting tonight's message comes from an NFL Coach. I remember him telling a newscaster that his job was to make certain that his team was in position at the end of the game to win. If the score was close in the final minutes victory still had a chance.

You are not going to win them all, but after 14 years of racing Michael McDowell found himself doing donuts in the winner's circle for one reason: **HE WAS IN POSITION** when it counted.

Here is a short video which will "drive" home today's message.
www.moreonseries.com/daytona

93. You Had Me At "Hello!"

I was reminded recently of a famous line in a movie with Tom Cruise and Renee Zellweger. The sound bite went viral with the line, **"You had me at hello."** This clearly endorsed the belief that first impressions are significant. (The movie was Jerry McQuire.

Let's see if I can share tonight's message without boring you to tears.

My wife and I are "thinking" about relocating to the west coast of Florida in the not-too-distant future. Last week we happened upon an attractive real estate development just a few miles north-east of Sarasota. We stopped in the Information Office and filled out a few forms indicating a sincere interest. I checked a box allowing future correspondence from real estate professionals.

Not unexpectedly, I soon received an email from a proactive agent offering assistance. I thought I would hear from others, but I guess I should not have been surprised. Most sales leads are never followed-up in a timely fashion regardless of the industry. (Hidden zing here.)

That particular email was followed by a voice message on my phone. Unlike many "tire-kickers" I wanted to explain my position to the agent as to not waste their time by misleading them. And here is where tonight's message kicks in.

I dialed the number left in the voice message and was connected to Matt. "Hello." "Hi. This is Mike Marchev." "Yes." "You emailed me earlier today and also left me a voice message on my phone." That is when it hit him. I could envision him seeing dollar signs flash before his eyes thinking he had a "live" one on the hook. His tone immediately changed.

I had initially given Matt high marks for following up. Little did he know he was dealing with a seasoned, experienced sales professional who had little patience for those who still gave credibility to their "gift-of-gab."

This man's decision to deliver his first impression by answering the phone like I was bothering him did little to establish a positive first impression. He definitely **DID NOT HAVE ME AT HELLO**. With very little effort he could have greeted me with just a little voice inflection and a modicum of personality while he ascertained who was calling.

I am betting that he is a good guy, and he can probably save me a lot of time as I continue my investigation of the west coast. But unknowingly, he took needless aim at shooting himself in the foot. Rumor has it that not unlike travel professionals, real estate agents grow on trees.

For selfish reasons, I am going to give this guy a little more rope to see if he is actually planning on hanging himself. (I hope he **"Snaps out of it"** and proves his value to me. (Another reference to another movie... Moonstruck with Cher and Nicholas Cage.)

The very first noise that exits your mouth, the very first time you look at somebody, the very first question you ask sets the tone and the stage for things to come. **Don't blow it.**

I want to share one more reminder with you tonight. First impressions (Hellos) are important to say the least. But last impressions are what people will remember. So although you may have me at hello, you better maintain your professional and personal decorum so you will keep me at good-bye.

*** You want more to think about? Check out my weekly podcast **(Mike'd Up Marchev)** at www.TraveMarketMedia.com Also listed on Spotify, Apple Podcasts, Google and iHeartRadio.

Update: I have since met with and worked with Matt. He did indeed snap out of it, and I am giving him high marks. In this case it worked out, but there are no guarantees when the initial impression falls short. You might not be given a second chance to redeem yourself.

94. Who Remembers The "E-Ticket?"

While writing tonight's article I was sitting in a Mastermind Meeting (Session Two) in Cancun, Mexico at the Grand Hotel at Moon Palace. This meeting had been on the books for over a year and had been cancelled twice since Covid-19 raised its ugly head. Originally scheduled for Jamaica, we decided to hold it in Mexico for logistics' sake.

It came as no surprise at the time that many people thought a trip to Mexico was less than intelligent. While never underestimating the severity of the pandemic, I have always endorsed the notion that "A ship is safe in a harbor... but that is not what ships are built for." At the time the pieces of the recovery puzzle were slowly coming together and I thought it was time to begin "thinking" again about getting out.

For me ... for us ... it was time to venture out and begin traveling again. Not without precautions. Not without mask protection. Not without social distancing. Not without showing respect for others.

At the half-way point of our Mastermind Retreat, we considered the first session to have been a success in every way. Southwest Airlines (my carrier) took the proper measures to ensure the safety of their passengers. The staff at The Grand could not have been any more professional, friendly, helpful and safety conscious.

Every guest was playing by the rules. Individual tables had been set up for each individual meeting participant with ample spacing between each seat. (8-10 feet.) The hotel had established a systematic COVID-19 testing procedure adhering to CDC requirements for re-entry to the United States.

In short, we were eager and ready for group #2 which was scheduled to arrive later that day.

Why am I telling you this? The world has been hit with a tremendous jolt for the past year but continues to spin. With the introduction of three vaccines (as of this writing) we are growing more confident that soon we will be looking back at this ugly sickness. People, at their own pace, will soon be returning to "their" lives as they once knew them. (Perhaps with a slightly different mindset.) Some people will take longer than others to readjust but that is okay. I am ready to start moving again, and this trip to Mexico proved to me that I had not made a foolish decision.

Stuart Cohen, myself and 22 professional travel entrepreneurs are beginning to climb back. In a sense, we are leading the way back to living our lives as we envision them to be. And we are here to help others do the same.

While writing tonight's story, I am not suggesting that the light has turned green and that it is full speed ahead. Far from it. It is not yet safe to "cast our fates to the wind." I am offering however, based on my current experiences, that the time is coming to get out and begin breathing some fresh air again.

The world will continue to spin with or without our approval. I am inviting you to consider jumping back on the carousel as soon as you are ready and join me in enjoying the only ride of your life.

You are currently holding your own "E-Ticket." If you do not use it, it is not transferable. My question to you is, "What are you planning to do with it?"

NOTE: Today's reference to the E-Ticket might bring you back to the Disney Booklet System where you had A, B, C, D and E-Tickets to enter rides and exhibits based on their considered value. The higher the letter, the more exhilarating the experience. **You are currently holding an "E -Ticket."**

95. What Are You Waiting For?

Last week before ending my Inner Circle sales meeting, I asked for opinions regarding my members' most pressing concerns. I should not have been surprised when I heard the response more often than not, being related to sales. After all, without sales you have no business. Without customers, you have nobody to service.

My mind shot to another recent response I received from those attending my Mastermind Owners Retreat in Cancun. The concern this group mentioned time and again involved the negative behavior referred to as **procrastination**. In preparing for tonight's story, I decided to couple these two concerns together.

I remember like it was yesterday the night I asked my undergraduate class of students at Fairleigh Dickinson University if after graduation they wanted to help people. The entire class responded with a resounding "yes." I then ask if they wanted to be their own boss after they graduated. Again, virtually 100% of the students answered in the affirmative. My third question involved their interest in making a lot of money. No surprises here. They all responded with hands raised instantly. I followed by asking them how many people after graduating were planning to become professional salespeople. Not one single hand went up. (Interesting, but not a surprise.)

The reason for this is simple. With very few exceptions, when you say the word "salesperson" the words manipulative, aggressive, liar, cheater, dishonest, car sales, insurance, closing tricks, up-selling, and overcoming objections shoot into one's mind.

It should come as no surprise that any person responsible for "selling" hesitates to ply their trade in fear that they will be categorized with any one or more of the negative terms listed above. I am not saying that many mis-guided sales "slugs" do not have less than admirable objectives. I do believe however, that a professional salesperson genuinely and sincerely has their client's interest in mind and can make a very comfortable living from helping people acquire what's in their best interest. Once this proactive mindset drives the actions of salespeople, *there is no need to procrastinate at all*.

One area where procrastination does raise its ugly head is associated with lead generation. It has always confused me when companies spend a significant amount of money generating leads and once their effort pays off, their salespeople find one million reasons why not to follow up expeditiously. (Very strange.)

It would be easy to refer to this lack of action as simply being lazy, but I have to think that it is connected with fear. The question *"what- if"* comes into play. What if they don't answer my phone call? What if they are not interested? What if they don't like my price? What if I call them at a bad time? What if they are just shoppers? **What if, what if, what if?**

Once we start asking ourselves **"what if"** questions it becomes easy to procrastinate and delay our next action since we do not want to become disappointed, rejected, dissed, or forlorn.

I think you know what's coming next. The sooner you identify your current (real) position in the world of your prospect the sooner you will be in position to respond appropriately.

We all procrastinate at times and I also fall into this rut. The truth is the sooner we address the truth and the reality of any single situation, the better we will feel, and the sooner we can deal with the pending situation. Sounds simple because it is simple.

The choice is yours. You can put off the inevitable, or as a popular shoe company reminds us, **"JUST DO IT."**

NOTE: If you are reading tonight's bedtime story, please send me an email and let me know how you are benefitting from reading this series of "stories." There are still five more coming your way. mike@mikemarchev.com

96. Playing Tentatively Is For Losers

I'd like to share a "moment" I had last week while talking to a professor from Montclair State University. Our common thread is that we both graduated from the University of Massachusetts. He specializes in Sports Psychology. I was a History Major but we both are now in the information business.

While holding my rapt attention, he asked me a question that immediately stopped me in my tracks. He asked me what was the worst thing any one of my athletic coaches could have said to me as I exited the field of play. I uttered some knee-jerk lame responses before asking him what he thought was the correct answer. **"Marchev. You look very tentative out there."**

Tentative is a word that implies hesitancy, caution, uncertainty, unsureness, and timidness. I don't know about you, but I am not a big fan of any of these synonyms. On the field of sport, or in the field of business the word timid holds little value.

This word opens up some very interesting discussions since you can also err on the flip side. Lawyers often do ... as do some doctors. Antonyms include: conceited, egotistical, unabashed, brash and fearless.

Not unlike doctors and lawyers, I have spent the last 35 years being paid for sharing my opinion. Thinking back, I may have teetered toward too much political correctness in fear that I might "upset" somebody. Yes, I very well might have come across as being "tentative."

And if this was the case, (and I am pretty sure it was the case) many people in my audiences had good cause to question the validity of my suggestions. If I spoke without an unwavering conviction, why should they drink my Kool-Aid?

I am not recommending that you offer anything but the truth, but I am inferring you do so with a firm and steadfast belief that your words are based on knowledge, experience and an unwavering focus toward the audience. If you have prepared properly and done your homework, there is no need for apologies or for treading lightly, walking on thin ice or weighing your words to extreme.

In your business, as in sport, there is little room for playing tentatively. Pedal to the medal. Full speed ahead. Leave everything you have on the field. Play hard. Have fun. And as my college football coach once reminded us, "If you don't know who to hit, hit somebody."

But whatever you do, do not do it **tentatively**.

97. Nobody Cares About You!

Tonight, I will end your day with a blinding flash of the obvious. **"Tomorrow is the FIRST day of the rest of your life."**

You can put the book down right now if you feel this is too elementary or lacks any pertinent substance. Like it or not ... endorse it or not ... it is as true as the nose on your face. Tomorrow is day one.

Tomorrow is when you can wipe the slate clean and start from square one. What you do with your time tomorrow it is entirely up to you. But be forewarned. In a few short hours, it will become "yesterday's news." Don't squander the opportunities that present themselves tomorrow.

For reasons I prefer not to share with you tonight, I woke up once again feeling like I got hit by a truck. When I peeked at the alarm clock and saw 5:45 am my back ached, my neck hurt, my legs felt numb and I could feel a slight twitch in my right ailing calf muscle. The sad news was this was nothing new. It was just another new day about to begin.

I managed to swing my legs off to the side of the bed and with a little leverage from my left arm I sat up and headed for the kitchen to perk a small pot of coffee. Each step was a focused work in progress. But as I usually do, I arrived safely at my destination and began scooping out the recommended amount of coffee per six cups of water.

Here comes the message. You don't give a hoot about my aching bones. Nor should you. You have enough problems of your own without having to conjure up any sympathy for my daily ailments.

Bottom Line: You don't care about me.

And as painful as this may sound, nobody cares about you. They have their own lives, concerns, dreams, problems, disappointments, challenges, regrets, aches, and pains. (Okay. If you are lucky maybe one or two people actually do care about your well-being. Especially those who figure they might have a line in your will.)

I am reminded of the old saying, **"Don't tell anybody your problems. 90% of those you tell don't care and the other ten percent are glad you have them."** You have a life to live, things to do, experiences to experience, and Pandemics to deal with. And you will. In your own formidable way. With style. With grace. With empathy and with intelligence. (Or you won't.)

But remember either way, nobody cares about you. You care about you. Press on. And there is no better day than tomorrow to begin a future you can be proud of.

I will continue to follow my morning regiment of stretching while eventually walking off the stiffness. And with any luck, by 10 am I will begin looking like a fully functioning human being. And I trust you will be doing the same. Stay safe and don't allow the naysayers in this world get you down. Misery loves company, and you don't want to be the next target.

98. Podcasts Have Become "The Talk Of the Town"

For the past nine months travel professionals have realized perhaps more than anybody that it was not the time to ply their trade. "Hunkering down" vs "Leaving town" became the norm.

Fast forward 280 days and these very same professionals are beginning to see the light at the end of the tunnel. The question now involves "how" to initiate interest again without appearing obnoxious, pushy, too edgy or manipulative. Enter the audio podcast.

Podcasts are not new. They have been available to inquisitive minds for years and now cover just about every topic or subject you can think of. And the time may be right for you to consider hosting your own travel-related podcast as a way to meaningfully re-enter your marketplace while establishing yourself as the knowledgeable source for information.

Although I hosted my first podcast years ago I recently jumped at the opportunity to work with Travel Research Online when they announced their new division - Travel Market Media. There are two reasons I am calling your attention to this resource today. First, to investigate the various podcasters at www.travmarketmedia.com to see the information available to you and to see if these podcasters can contribute to your ongoing professionalism. Second, to get a good idea of how these podcasts are presented and to envision you as a future host of your own topic-specific show.

I invite you to check out my new podcast titled **Mike'd Up Marchev**. I decided to keep my programs short realizing you have a zillion other tasks on your daily to-do list. Take a peek at **https://tinyurl.com/kkp7vcuw** and listen to a few of the pre-recorded episodes.

What is of particular interest about these podcasts is that they can be distributed a number of ways. Mine can be found on ITunes, Spotify and IHeartRadio by searching **Mike'd Up Marchev**. This allows me to communicate with interested listeners all over the world. And yes, you can too.

COVID-19 may not be a thing of the past quite yet, but you can still begin spreading the good word again while positioning yourself as the "real deal." Podcasting just might be what you have been waiting for.

99. Playing It Safe May Not Be Your Best Move

My early experience with "failure" conjures up painful memories of my Little League Baseball days. At age nine I was introduced to the agony of defeat without a single opportunity to enjoy the thrill of victory. That year the "Hawks" went 0-20, and that was the year our team learned that life was not always fair. Unlike today's losing teams, we did not receive a trophy for simply "showing up." or knowing how to correctly position a baseball cap. We watched as our friends received the accolades they appropriately deserved.

Without blaming our performance on a lack of skill or perhaps our poor competitive spirit, I think "failure," when analyzed properly, remains the quickest path to future success. I happen to be one who endorses failure as the quickest way to achieve a pre-determined objective. The motto I have shared on more than one occasion is, ***"Fail your way to success."*** *(*I might add that I do not suggest that you fail "stupid.")

But many adults shy away from the embarrassment associated with failure by avoiding challenges that may appear risky at first glance. The "safe" thing to do has always been to "fit in" to the establishment. To be a good "doobie." How boring is that? And you call yourself an entrepreneur!

The phrase that I thought of when reading this passage was "social acceptance." Even at a young age we wanted to look like, act like, and be admired by our peers. At the time we felt cool when we were considered a member of the in-crowd. Times have changed. Situations have changed. Normal behavior has changed. How to stay in business has changed.

Step away from the "same-ole-same-ole" rank and file. Don't be a duck following the lead of the head duck. Take your place in the fast lane. Take a risk. Roll the dice. Believe in yourself and your instincts. Be an eagle. (Eagles don't flock.)

Be you.

100. "You've Got This!"

I was reminded of these three words while watching a TV show a few months back. It hit a chord with me, and I decided to adopt it as my new "phrase that pays." Stay with me as I explain the significance behind these words.

I will tell you one thing right from the start. These words and the associated "belief" that come with them have nothing to do with hoping, wishing, dreaming, and any inherent optimism you might possess. The mere utterance of these three words will do little to make your "dream" a reality.

In my case, I repeat these three words to myself when I am feeling tired, frustrated or finding myself wanting to quit my daily training routine. You have heard me say numerous times that "the mind quits first." And when I find my mind wanting to "quit," I simply say to myself, *"I've got this."*

But here is the **"only"** way this phrase can pay dividends. It works because I know I have put in the hours, the repetitions, the laps, the miles, the pains and the mental preparation that supports this personal belief without exception. After paying the price you can say with conviction **"I've got this."** And I might add, you will not only hear yourself saying it but you will feel refreshed and exhilarated knowing it is the truth.

Okay. I set the stage using my current situation as an example. Let's see how this all pertains to you and your personal travel business.

Before you can adopt these three words as your "phrase that pays," you have to get yourself into a position that warrants the belief. Here are a few questions that might help your pending action plan.

1. Have you cemented relationships with your short list of "A" Clients?
2. Have you weeded out (discarded) the bottom feeders? Those clients that are draining your energies and profits.
3. Are your current supplier relationships up to date?
4. Have you decided on a specialty? (Niche?)
5. If applicable, do you know what motivates your employees?
6. (**Backup**.) Do you know what motivates YOU?
7. Do you know your marketing message? Do you believe it?
8. Do you have a plan designed to rekindle former accounts?
9. If applicable, do you have a consistent and programmed communication vehicle?
10. Have you decided what conferences/seminars you will attend in the next 12 months?
11. Do you know how you will celebrate that next big piece of business?
12. Do you honestly have the good of your customers as your primary concern?

If you are still reading, I know what is going through your mind. You are thinking this is starting to sound a lot like a New Year's Marketing Plan. And it is already April. But if there is any truth to the saying, **"Tomorrow is the first day of the rest of your life,"** then this "shoe" just might fit.

To me, tonight's article is both logical and timely. I am paying my dues "daily" to make sure I am ready when May15th arrives when I am waiting to begin the swim in Panama City Beach. I will be mentally and physically prepared to say without hesitation, **"I've got this."**

In your world when you feel your stress quotient begin to rise for any one of a million legitimate reasons, you will know you have prepared diligently and are ready to "do your thing." You will be the right person for the job since you will know, and believe in all your heart, that **"You've got this."**

My Final Words!

I am assuming you finished reading more than a few of the stories, lessons, reminders and suggestions shared in this book. This in and of itself, speaks volumes as to your genuine interest in bettering yourself and your business.

You might want to return to the **Table of Contents** and glance through the 100 stories and click on a few titles to solidify the messages that were specifically talking to you.

For many of you, the information you have just reviewed is enough to keep you busy and focused for months. For others, you may need a little more help to keep you pointed in the right direction. Perhaps you are seeking a little "accountability."

For the past eight years (maybe a few more) I have assembled a group of proactive travel professionals and like-minded entrepreneurs. We call ourselves **The Inner Circle** and we meet every two weeks online.

We have a resource library; a private Facebook Group; and all members have immediate access to my opinions and experience along with their personal questions and concerns. But the primary selling feature of membership is the fact that we meet every two weeks to energize our creativity and share best practices. I strongly recommend that you give this group a try.

Send me an email at mike@mikemarchev.com with the words **Inner Circle** in the subject box. I will fill in all the unknowns for you so you can better decide if participation in my Inner Circle is for you.

Okay. I shared. You read. You slept. Now it is time to put a few of these ideas into motion. It's Showtime. I know **"you've got this."**

Mike Marchev

Mike's Bio

Like you, Mike has seen the word "sales" bandied about in numerous ways over the years. Definitions suggest the "gift-for-gab, closing, up-selling and the knack for overcoming customer objections." Flamboyancy, resilience, and a thick skin usually complete the picture. Maybe this all pertained to yesterday's sales professional, but certainly not today.

With over three decades of selling, teaching, speaking, and more importantly, real-life, in-the-trenches sales experience, Mike's views are radically refreshing. He believes that sales involves personal connection and that sales remains a "contact sport."

Mike is known for his practical, street-savvy delivery. His fusion of real-life stories with his conversational presentation style makes it easy to connect with his audiences.

Unlike many of today's speakers who attempt to leverage negative experiences or glowing accomplishments into meaningful messages, Mike has taken a circuitous route through his career building up an arsenal of true-life examples which are appreciated and easily identified with. (The fact that he is a single-engine airplane pilot, a certified Coast Guard sailing captain, an Ironman Triathlete and a fun-loving business practitioner tends to lend interest to his many humorous but meaningful business messages and personal stories.)

From University Teaching Experience to International Sales Management; from Entrepreneur to Professional Speaker, Mike has developed the skill to connect with audiences on all levels in ways that induce a real and genuine behavior change.

The author of the popular sales book Become The Exception and founder of the "More-On" Business Development Series, Mike continues to share his provocative insights with online E-zines, Podcasts, blogs and industry business magazines.

His clients include: AmaWaterways, Vacation.com, Travel Leaders, Travel Savers, Carlson Wagonlit, Uniglobe, Travel Research Online, MAST, National Business Travel Association, Meeting Planners International, ASTA, HERTZ, AT&T, Johnson & Johnson, Siemens, Sysco Foods, Wells Fargo Bank, Toyota, Pitney Bowes, Merck, Nextel, Los Alamos National Labs, The Washington Post and American Express to name a few.

Prior to his speaking career, Mike sold electronic components for a large New Jersey based manufacturing company leading to international sales experience. Before heading down the entrepreneurial path on his own, Mike worked for the highly respected Maritz Company, a successful motivation and communications company headquartered in St. Louis. Mike earned his Masters Degree in Marketing from Fairleigh Dickinson University after graduating from the University of Massachusetts with a B.A. in History.

As the president and founder of HeadFirstSales Mike spends the majority of his working hours sharing proven sales methods to proactive entrepreneurs. The travel and hospitality industry has been his primary focus for the past thirty years. **100 Bedtime Stories For Travel Professionals** is his latest project designed to motivate travel entrepreneurs to maximize their inherent abilities to grow a successful travel business in times of unprecedented challenge. At the time of this writing, Mike was training for a 70.3 Ironman Triathlon at age 72.

www.ingramcontent.com/pod-product-compliance
Lightning Source LLC
Chambersburg PA
CBHW080926220526
45465CB00008BA/2943